The
Exceptional
Manager!

Tools to Help Build Up Your Business and Develop Your People

KEITH LARSON

PORTLAND • OREGON
INKWATERPRESS.COM

www.inkwaterpress.com

ISBN-10 1-59299-282-X
ISBN-13 978-1-59299-282-9

Publisher: Inkwater Press

Printed in the U.S.A.
All paper is acid free and meets all ANSI standards for archival quality paper.

This book is dedicated to the four women in my life and to the managers that want to make a difference.

To my wife, Sharon, who is my soul mate forever!

To my daughters, Krystal & Nicole. I hope my experiences in this book help you to be even more successful in life.

To my mother, Silly Sally, who passed away this last year. May her spirit live in my wife and daughters.

To all the managers who find passion in their work and want to build up their businesses. I hope this book gives them the needed skills to develop and to grow their teams and businesses to their full potential.

TABLE OF CONTENTS

Section One – Build the Business

Section Two – Developing the People

INTRODUCTION

You went to school to learn a skill. Maybe you received a degree in Accounting, Engineering, Law, Design, Fashion, Marketing, Science, Medicine, Nursing, Business, etc., and were just promoted to management. Or you may *not* have a degree but have worked very hard at your job for years and have now been promoted to management. Many companies put people in leadership or managerial positions just because they've done their job well. This might be the right decision, but the problem is that the new promotion is usually not followed by management training. A strong passion for management training will make sure it gets done. Good management training will help a new manager be more successful. A successful manager will help the people and the business grow. Find the passion for training and development to help *your* business—and *your* people—grow.

Conventional wisdom talks about leaders being born and not made. This is a very debatable statement and not in the scope of this book. However, all new managers, whether they are born leaders or not, need support and training to be successful in their new position. A newly promoted manager probably has the support network at work or she or he would not have been promoted. Very few companies in today's pressure-packed business environment have the time, energy, or money to develop a manager's training guide and train their new managers.

Many experienced managers need support also—a little help, perhaps, in building their business to the next stage or in developing their people. Over the last few years it seems like a lot of managers have been promoted who end up tearing apart the business or concentrating on the short-term profits or even their own gains only. **The Exceptional Manager builds the business and develops the people. Business today can sure use more Exceptional Managers**

of departments or the overall business. Have the courage to be an Exceptional Manager. You have a major influence on your people's careers and their lives. There is no such thing as the perfect manager. However, if you build up your business and develop your people, you will exceed your expectations.

The purpose of this book is to give both the newly promoted and the experienced manager a guide to becoming an Exceptional Manager. Today's fast-paced business climate dictates a new approach to management—an easy-to-learn and easy-to-apply, no-fail system to managing your responsibilities. Even in the rush for success, a manager can develop the business and the people within it. The proven approach outlined in this book can take some time but it has a fast payback, accelerating actual results. Be an Exceptional Manager and develop your business and your people for short-term and long-term success. Have the courage to make a difference.

The Strategic Planning Cycle:
A Process to Build the Business

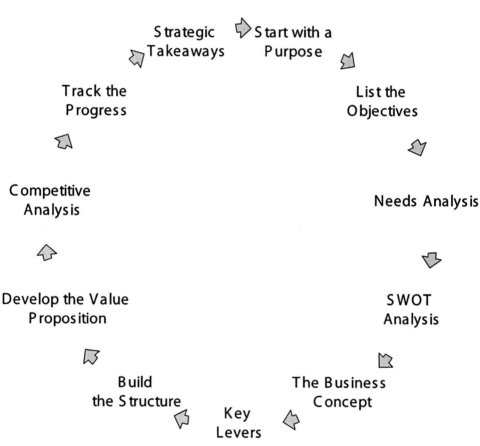

Strategic Takeaways

Start with a Purpose

Track the Progress

List the Objectives

Competitive Analysis

Needs Analysis

Develop the Value Proposition

SWOT Analysis

Build the Structure

Key Levers

The Business Concept

Chapter One

DEVELOPING THE BUSINESS PURPOSE

Every business has a purpose and it is usually or almost always to make money. This is the right purpose but is it enough to just make money? It seems that a lot of employees want a better direction than just striving for money. Most employees want to make a difference, and since they spend most of their lives at work, why shouldn't they make a difference there? If managers can engage this desire in their employees, and channel it properly, it will help the business.

Even the statement that the business purpose is "to make money" probably will not help the business achieve that goal. A business purpose should describe more of the business's overall goals, and it should lay them out clearly. There are 4-5 key messages that a business purpose should cover. **Figure 1** gives an example that covers the 4-5 key elements of a good business purpose. It is important to the employees, shareholders, stakeholders, vendors, and customers to understand what the business is all about.

The **first step** (**Figure 1, item 1**) to a solid business purpose is to describe what the commitment to the business is about. Is it important to make a lot of products? Is quality of the product the key business's competitive advantage? Is this a service business? Is this a low-cost provider business? A research and development business? There is no right or wrong answer as long as the first purpose is the truth and it is the real competitive advantage or the real reason the business is successful. The example says that the purpose of the business is "**To deliver high quality products that always surpass the customer's expectations.**" This is a much different purpose than other companies might have, such as: "To always be the low-cost producer in every market that we are involved in." This is a strong statement to the businesses and the customers!

The **second step** in developing a business purpose is to make a commitment to the employees. These are the people that really make the business come alive and achieve its vision and purpose. The statement here needs a lot of thought before it is written down. The manager of a business is making a commitment to the employees that they will see every day. If this statement is not well thought out or is not really supported, the employees will know right away. It is better to have no statement than one that is not supported. The question that needs to be answered in this purpose statement is, "What is the real commitment to the people?"

There are several ways to show the organization's commitment to its employees. The commitment statement is a good start, and should be written for the present business environment. This important statement cannot make an empty promise, such as promising long-term employment when that option is not possible. The **Figure 1** example statement in **bullet point number two** tries to be clear on the short-term and long-term commitment to the employees. The statement, **"To provide stable employment and future growth opportunities,"** clearly makes a commitment to try to give the employees a steady paycheck so they can pay their bills, and at the same time give them opportunities for growth in the future. This statement is not—nor can it be—a guarantee of employment now or in the future; the world of work in today's economy makes it almost impossible to give any guarantees. But this purpose statement makes a commitment to establish stability and growth as goals the company can try to provide for their employees.

The third commitment that is critical to every business is the one the organization makes to its **investors**. Every organization has investors who are key to getting the organization off the ground. No organization would get off the ground without some seed money. These funds can come from several different sources, like a private investor, the entrepreneur's life's savings, the stock market, etc. No matter where the money comes from to start, sustain, and grow an organization, there is always a need to get a return on the investment. There is a long list of requirements from investors. They might want a quick return on their investment. Some might not even want a financial return but would be satisfied to see a cause come true. Whatever the needs of the investors, those needs have to be clear to the organization. The expectations of the investors need to be written down and agreed to. If there is a misunderstanding, major problems will soon surface. An investor can withdraw support very quickly and then the organization is really vulnerable. The **third bullet point** in the purpose statement shows the commitment to the investors. It says, **"To return a high profit margin on growing sales for business sustainability and financial stability."** The commitment to the investors can take several avenues but it must be clear and agreed to by them.

The next key commitment is to the business itself. How is the business going to make itself a sustainable business? What are the key drivers (see **Chapter 8**) to make the business successful now and in the future? It is critical to find those key drivers that lead to success and to clarify them for the organization. Once those key drivers are known, management must make a commitment to the organization and everyone involved. The key drivers must continue to get funding and support.

The key drivers of the example in **Figure 1** describe a commitment to research and development when it says **"To develop a constant pipeline of creative new products."** The organization in this example is a creative company that is dependent on new products to sustain its business now and in the future. Most people in this organization probably know how important new products are, but it makes a strong impression on everyone to make a clarifying statement of support. If it is very clear, through this purpose, that one of the most important elements of this company is a constant pipeline of new products, then the key people will know they are supported.

The final purpose of this example is the commitment of the organization to its suppliers and community. No organization can survive without constant, reliable, and competitively priced goods and services that meet the needs of the business. Many times the supplier is an afterthought; at others, the supplier is taken advantage of. However, just try living for a short time without the critical supplies. Most organizations have more than one supplier for every one of their needs. In today's competitive world, there are probably suppliers standing in line to take the place of one who fails. However, organizations that work very closely with a supplier and are respectful of its needs can find efficiencies and cost savings that might not have been thought possible. The same is true about the communities in which an organization is located. If the business has a great reputation in the community, it will attract better employees and get better treatment from that community when it needs support. The statement in **bullet point five** tries to tell the vendors, the community, and the organization that the vendors and the community are important for survival: **"To be a good partner with all stakeholders including the community & the vendors."**

Business Purpose
Figure 1

The Purpose of the *Business* is:

1) To deliver high quality products which always surpass our customers' expectations.
2) To provide stable employment and new opportunities for our employees.
3) To achieve a high profit margin on growing sales for business sustainability and financial stability.
4) To develop a constant pipeline of creative new products.
5) To be a good partner with all stakeholders including the community & the vendors.

Chapter Two

DEVELOPING BUSINESS OBJECTIVES

A business needs goals for the next 3-5 years. This may seem like long-term goals in today's world but 5-10 years is really a long-term timeframe. A business should also have yearly goals. Yearly goals are usually set to have the business hit its yearly budget. A 3-5 year plan is made to have the business execute over a longer timeframe but it is not, in most cases, long enough to retool the organization. The purpose of setting 3-5 year goals is to establish a vision from which is created a multiyear plan to significantly improve the business. The objectives in **Figure 2** are set to help the business dramatically improve over 3 years in several areas. Most organizations have at least one company goal for every major functional area. There is usually at least one goal for sales, operations, human resources, finance, legal, research and development, and most organizations should have a goal in the international area.

The example in **Figure 2** tries to have at least one goal for most major functional areas as described above. The **first bullet point** focuses on sales. If a business does not have a strong sales strategy, there may be no need to have other objectives. One shoe does not fit every organization in this area. Some organizations want and need to grow and grow fast. The growth objective should be stated in their objectives. Some organizations just want to stop the bleeding and minimize the constant reduction in sales. Both cases are valid and both could be desired performance given the present markets for each. In both cases, the organization must have a plan of how to deal with the present 3-5 year conditions. This example is for an organization that has chosen to

"have double digit percent sales increases every year" (sales increases of 10% or higher for every year in the plan).

Process efficiencies are critical and necessary every year. The process could be manufacturing, retail, product development, healthcare, legal, and more. No matter what the business is, process efficiency cannot be avoided. If a company wants to survive, constant improvement is necessary; this is a goal that never goes away. The number of process efficiency improvements might change every year and might vary based on the organization. The market and the level of business maturity will determine the amount of constant change required. Every organization must improve every year. The **second bullet point** in the example tries to show how a process efficiency goal can be stated. It says that its goal is to **"Improve the process efficiencies by 5% every year in order to maintain and improve the margins during this fast growth phase."**

The second section of this book will really help the new or even the experienced manager achieve goals in the human resource area. Sometimes these goals are hard to set because many of them are hard to make time-bounded and measurable. The example in **Figure 1, point 3,** tries to set human resource goals that can be measured. These goals are listed to help set the foundation of a new or an old organization that needs to be revamped. Organizations that have good human resource systems in place might want to set goals that improve the productivity of people or set goals that reduce the people-cost in the system or costs per dollar of sales.

Goals need to be set for the research and development teams also. It is very hard to set realistic goals for the R&D team. New products are not developed linearly because most of the time new products come in surges. There may not be any progress for a long time and then suddenly there is a breakthrough and a bunch of new ideas and products come to light. This does not mean that the R&D team has free reign to develop new products on their timeline. The R&D team must have goals, and try very hard to reach those goals, since the organization needs new products in order to survive. The best way to set goals in this area is to make them broad, like the **fourth bullet point** in **Figure 2**. As the goal states, the team should develop a product pipeline that adds four new products per year.

Most finance departments are scorekeepers but they have a lot more to give an organization than just adding up the numbers. The accounting and finance departments are very good with numbers and they know the costs of the organization. They can be great allies with the rest of the organization by helping them identify cost reduction opportunities. The finance department can also find opportunities themselves either in their own department or in others.

The final major goal area in this example is the international area. Almost every company should have an international goal because the world really has gone global. If the organization does not need or want an international department, it can survive in some cases—but not in most. New managers might not have any responsibility for the international business but a manger might be newly promoted to the international organization. Also, a new manager might have a department goal that supports the international department. The international team should get strong support from all the other departments.

The terms "goals" and "objectives" are used interchangeably by design. These terms are usually the exact same in practice and in this book. Goals should be objective in nature and measurable. They should also have specific delivery completion dates wherever possible.

Business Objectives
Figure 2
Example

The main goals of the business over the next 3 years are:

1) Increase double digit percent sales every year.

2) Improve the process efficiencies by 5% every year in order to maintain and improve the margins during this fast growth phase.

3) Develop the appropriate human resource systems including an internal communication system, a formal pay system, and a performance evaluation & development system.

4) Finalize and implement at least four new products.

5) Establish a finance department that contributes to the core business by finding savings of at least $500,000 over the plan period.

6) Establish a robust international business by enlisting two major new customers per year.

Chapter Three

NEEDS ANALYSIS:
WHAT IT TAKES & WHY

The first place to look when building or rebuilding a business—or even a department—is the market. Many times an organization looks internally first. It is a lot easier to influence the business than it is to change the market, so a lot of businesses take the path of least resistance and go after internal change first and look at the market second. It might be easier to reduce internal costs, but the first analysis must be on the competition and the market. If the first focus is on internal actions, the changes might make good but in all the wrong places. Inappropriate actions within the business can happen for the company manager or for a department manager. A new manager of a department must analyze the internal competition first. Then, the manager must look into the contribution this department makes to the overall business or to the sales. Finally, the manager must develop a plan for the department. The following describes the chart in **Figure 3.**

<u>Branding</u> – There are plenty of books to help a manager develop a brand for their products or for the company overall. The key here is to recognize what is really important about the business. Some companies have made every product or service stand on its own and have a unique brand for everything. Some companies use one brand name and then add other products and services under that product brand umbrella. The leaders of the organization must choose the strategy after a lot of input, and then a detailed plan can follow. The same is true internally. What is the desired reputation of the internal department? Is it a support department that helps other

departments with stellar ideas and services? What is an internal department's brand?

Marketing and Promotion – What is the market share that an organization is striving for? Does the business have a strategy to be Number 1 or 2 in every market that they compete in, or does it want to carve out a niche? After a determination of the desired market share is developed, the marketing and promotional strategies, budget, and actions can be developed. The same is true for the new department manager. The new manager has decided what the purpose and objectives of the business or department are. The new manager has decided what the department's brand should be. Now the new manager must decide how to promote that internal department. Internal marketing does not use a large budget and typical advertising. This promotion can be subtle, like getting the word out on how good the department is at helping by immediately fixing a major problem.

Strong Sales Force – How are the products of a business going to be sold? Some businesses sell over the internet, some use the push sales person who really goes after the sale in a high-pressure fashion. Some businesses use retail outlets. Some sales forces just build long-term relationships and believe that the sales will follow as the relationships mature. The product or service that is being sold really dictates what sales strategy will work best. An organization might use every one of the sales force options described above or it might only use one or even an option that is not listed. The question is, "What will it take to sell the product or service successfully?" The internal department manager must do the same analysis on a smaller scale. How is the department manager going to get the word out on his department and what it can deliver? What can be done to make the organization see the skills and services that the new manager's department will deliver?

Product Pipeline – The market is very dynamic and the competition fierce. A product or service's life cycle is much shorter today than even a few years ago. International competition has changed the face of the market. A new product on the market now can face competition from many different angles. The competition will come from the traditional markets and also from the emerging markets. New fashion trends or new technology may also shorten a product life cycle. New products and services must be ready for a quick introduction if and when the present products start to wind down. Having a product and service pipeline filled with new products, services, and customers will help an organization to be ready for the future. The same is true for a department. If a department has helped in the past to make the overall organization stronger, then it might need to come up with new ideas on how to help the organization in new ways in the future.

Smart Pricing – Product or service pricing is one of the hardest and most important decisions that an organization has to deal with. Many times an organization looks at their cost structure, adds on the margin that they desire, and sets the product or service price based on the costs plus strategy. This approach hardly ever works unless there is little or no competition. Most businesses have to look at their cost structure but also review the market pricing. It is critical to the organization to come up with pricing at a point where they can make money and where they are positioned in the market so the consumer believes that the product or service has value at the established price. The same is true internally. An internal department's time and resources are not free. Some companies have internal cross-charging for services and some just provide an internal service without a direct charge. However, even though the service is supposedly free, it might be part of the overhead charge or may not be charged at all. Either way, an internal service will eventually have to justify its price in the internal market. A department must be perceived also as adding value for the internal "price" of its service.

Competitive Awareness – What is the competition doing? There is an entire chapter devoted to competitive analysis in this book. The company that blinks and does not keep totally aware of what the competition is doing will lose. The competition is not only the direct products or markets that the organization competes in; competition can come from a completely unanticipated area. What product can completely replace music CDs? Maybe it is an MP3 player. The CD manufacturer might be in a business of the past or in a significantly reduced market. To a new department manager, the exact same is true. Many new managers don't even think about internal competition. What if another department wants to absorb this new manager's department? If this happens, there will be no job for the department. What if there is a similar department internally and they are threatened by the new manager? The other department may want to eliminate the future internal competition before the new manager gets his feet on the ground and well-positioned.

Field Follow-up – A product or service is only as good as how well it is serviced. Even if the product is built to last, a customer wants to have a place to contact the company for questions or service. Service can be on the phone, the internet, email, field service representatives, or a customer service department. The message that follow-up gives may be the only message the customer gets from the company. Some companies do surveys as part of the follow-up, some do follow-up through informal conversations, and some just don't do anything. The key for the organization is to think about what message it wants to give and what follow-up it can afford. If the organization does not address this issue, it will get field follow-up by default—which may not be what it wants. The same is true of the internal organization. A new manager should constantly be following up with his internal customers to find out how their internal services are rated.

A High Sense of Urgency – A person only gets so many opportunities to make a major contribution or a positive impression. Some people get a few more opportunities and some businesses a few more chances, but if those opportunities are not recognized or taken advantage of, they are squandered; not only may they never come again, but they might even lead to disaster for a person or an organization. This is true internally for a new manager. The best opportunity for the new manager and her new department might come the first day she is on the job. A high sense of urgency is always important for people, departments, and organizations.

This does not mean that they should work fast or recklessly, but that they must always be prepared and have a need to achieve the desired results.

The Right State of Mind – The entire second section of this book is about getting the organization in the right state of mind to do business. A team with the right mindset takes care of business and gets the right things done and done well.

Needs Analysis
Figure 3

What It Requires	*Why*
Branding	The brand name is a quality promise to your customers.
Marketing & Promotion	Your products need a share of the market; customer awareness is key.
Strong Sales Team	What is the best sales channel? Push sales, retail, the internet or relationship selling.
Product Pipeline	Trends and fashions shape products demand; fresh ideas win.
Smart Pricing	What are the prices for similar products? Prices are set by the market, not costs.
Competitive Awareness	Margins are driven by product superiority or low cost actions. What will others do?
Field Follow-up	What actions are required to support your products or services in the markets?
A High Sense of Urgency	There are only so many opportunities; timing is of the essence. You need to be ready to act.
The Right State of Mind	A strong team with a positive attitude takes care of business.

Chapter Four

ASSESSING THE RISKS & OPPORTUNITIES

A good way for the new manager of a company or of a department to understand the challenges and necessary actions of the future is to do an assessment of the risks and opportunities. This assessment should be done as soon as possible. It should be an easy exercise. There will be plenty of employees in the company or department that will want to give input. There will be a lot of great ideas—and also some bad ones. The exercise should be open to getting as many ideas as possible. All of the ideas can be filtered down to the best ones later on. Another source for good ideas can be all the stakeholders, such as the customers, vendors, investors, community members, and even competitors if they are accessible. There will also be information on the industry from the internet or publications. It might help to talk to people that have nothing to gain, such as random people in the community.

This brainstorming exercise is a very valid process to get a long list of ideas. It is not appropriate for this same group to try and evaluate which are the best ideas or most important. There are too many personal agendas in an organization, and with stakeholders, to get unbiased recommendations. Investors will think their ideas are most important and employees will think theirs best. A small group of senior managers must decide on the biggest risks and opportunities. The following is an example list of potential risks and opportunities with an explanation of each. The risks and opportunities should cover a wide range of business functional areas because there are probably risks and opportunities in many different areas.

Risks

- **Missing New Opportunities** – There will be many new opportunities and maybe even more opportunities than the organization can follow up on. There will have to be a vehicle for finding the best new ideas and getting them evaluated. Maybe an internal focus group or weekly meetings with the R&D team.

- **Not Funding Cost Reductions** – Some organizations or departments promote the same type of person and the team becomes focused on only one or a few areas. Some teams will only focus on similar new ideas and miss unusual cost-saving opportunities.

- **Missing Financial Targets** – The investors and the banks will always watch the new manager of a company, or maybe even a department, more closely at the beginning. He is an unproven entity. If the bank covenants, the budget, or investor requirements are missed at the beginning of a manager's reign, the risk of management changes will dramatically increase.

- **Trying to Do Too Many Things at Once** – A new person wants to prove herself—especially at the beginning—but it is best to be careful. Most organizations will put more weight on her ability to achieve what she says she can do. It is almost always better to set challenging goals, but not too high. If you set the goals at a reasonable level, and achieve those goals, it is much better than setting high goals and not achieving them.

- **New Product Pipeline Not Replenished** – One of the easiest ways to save money is to cut the marketing or the product development budgets. An organization might be able to get away with product development cost-cutting for a short time, but this will catch up with it. If product sales slow down unexpectedly, and there is nothing in the pipeline to replace them, there will be big problems.

- **Employee Turnover, Bad Employee Training, or the Wrong Employee Count** – Employee issues can cause an organization a lot of trouble. If there is an excess amount of turnover, the organization will have a hard time implementing its plan since the players keep changing. If there are too few people, the organization will have a hard time getting enough resources to do more than getting the core business done. If there are too many employees, the cost will be too high and there might not be enough work to keep the employees utilized; too little work can lead to more politics.

Opportunities

- **New Production Opportunities** – A new production method could improve the overall business' efficiencies. Any improvement in efficiencies will improve the company's bottom line and will increase its new funds for areas that need them.

- **Line Extension Opportunities** – All good brands have outstanding reputations. Taking the brand name and using it for another product or service that may or may not be similar or associated with the brand can help sales. A line extension strategy could lead to some immediate opportunities since a new product might gain market acceptance right away by getting carried along on the brand's shirttails. A solid brand name can help one or more products, but if those line extensions are not very strong they could hurt the brand name.

- **International Expansion** – There are very few businesses that should not consider taking their product or service to the international market. With the way the internet can handle ordering, product information, and even service implementation, a good product can be used almost anywhere. Rolling out a product or service internationally can be expensive and many organizations have a hard time funding the expansion. Developing an affiliation with an international partner might be a cost-effective way to expand internationally.

- **New Product or Service Introductions** – One of the best opportunities that an organization can take advantage of is a new product or service introduction. The new manager of a company or department should ask the team immediately what products or services are in development that have potential and can be expedited to market. Many times there are products that get bogged down in an organization for many reasons. These products might just need a champion to bring them to market. The only fear is to bring a product or service to market before it is ready, even if it is expedited carefully.

- **Generating New Ideas** – There are a lot of sources for new ideas. The new ideas can come from new employees, present employees, vendors, past employees, competitors, focus groups—the list goes on forever. A new manager should have a reputation for accepting new ideas, especially since he might be new to the job.

- **Refreshing Old Products** – Many products or services get tired when there is no new investment in their development, advertising, or promotion. Just a simple new advertising campaign, a new product enhancement, or even a small product or service promotion will give new life to an old product or service. This might be the best and fastest way to get new revenue.

- **Supplier Cost Reductions** – Companies talk a lot about partnerships with their supplier but it seems like there are not very many companies that actually partner well with their suppliers. Suppliers know a lot about the companies they support. They know about the products, services, people, and—maybe most importantly—the competition. They can give a lot of ideas to an organization without breaking confidentiality. They can also help reduce overall product costs if they are brought into the process as a true partner in the business.

- **New Sales Channels** – Strong companies, and even weak companies, have good sales channels but they might have sales channels that are not productive or not as productive as they could be. There are so many sales channels in the market today that there are, likewise, many options. A sales channel could be the normal routes like retail store, the internet, or distributors, but there are many others that a lot of people do not consider strongly enough. A sales channel can come through a partnership, a package bundling opportunity, an industrial channel for a consumer product, etc.

Risks & Opportunities
Figure 4

Risks	Opportunities
• Missing new product opportunities	• New production cost or efficiency introductions
• Not finding cost reduction or efficiency opportunities	• Product line extensions
• Missing financing covenants	• International expansion
• Trying to roll out too many opportunities at once	• New product or service introductions
• New product pipeline not being replenished	• Present employees' new ideas
• Key employee turnover	• New employees' new ideas
• New employees added too fast or too slow	• Refreshing old products
• New employee training not in place	• Supplier cost reductions
	• New sales channels

Chapter Five

STRENGTHS, WEAKNESSES, OPPORTUNITIES & THREATS ANALYSIS

Business moves at the speed of light. Many times a business has to change before a study is completed and its recommendations implemented. It is very appropriate to do as much research as possible and make decisions based on facts. If the pace of the business allows complete research, then the business should be patient for the results of that research and implement the recommendations after the facts are in. Most business managers for the company and for the departments in the company cannot afford to wait for the results of in-depth studies. Many businesses have to collect the best information in the shortest time and then make key decisions on imperfect data.

A **SWOT** (Strengths, Weaknesses, Opportunities & Threats) analysis is a best guess analysis but it can be very helpful. The best way to do the SWOT analysis is to gather the people who are the closest to the business. These people are probably a combination of the senior management, the key sales and technical people, and the human resource and finance teams. Other great resources are the product development, marketing, and production teams. The hourly people in the business usually have a lot to offer a SWOT analysis since they see the business from a different perspective than management does.

The next step is to take the target people mentioned above and have them answer a very simple form which asks for the biggest strengths, weaknesses, opportunities, and threats from their perspective. Hopefully, this task should develop a long list of ideas. Then, management should narrow the list down to the top 6 to 8 in each category. This exercise is not a voting exercise. If it were a voting exercise, the management team might be cautious about who to involve. The bigger the list the harder it will be to narrow it down. The senior management of the company or the department is always responsible for the results. Management needs to make the final decisions and not abdicate its authority to a vote. The input should be organized by each section; then the management team can see the entire input and perspective of all the people who participated.

The strengths area is the simplest area to start with since these ideas come very easily to the people in the business. People are usually very proud of where they work and instantly think of all the great things that they and the company do. The problem for the manager is to find the true strengths of the organization since the input from the people within it will definitely be biased. Many people will think that their department is the biggest strength of the organization, and not every department is the key to the business.

Figure 5 is an example of collecting the input from several people and trying to sort the information into the top strengths. This is an important exercise since the key information will be used to make the organization stronger. This exercise is critical to the organization's development in the way that a performance appraisal is very important to the development of an individual. A plan will need to be developed on all four of these key areas. The **Strengths** of the organization will need to be supported and enhanced. A plan on how to use the strengths is very important to the business. The **Weaknesses** will need immediate attention to minimize the negative impact that can happen on their account. The organization's **Opportunities** are actually the first thing the management team will focus on; a plan to go after the key opportunities will help implement those opportunities as soon as possible. There are only so many opportunities and so much money within an organization, so the management team must select the right opportunities and make sure they are not wasted. The key opportunities must get implemented.

Strengths – The organization has a core competency. These are the
skills that are unique or somewhat unique to the business. The core

competencies are critical so they can be used to drive an organization to the next level. Some organizations wander away from their core competencies and then end up in trouble. The business is suddenly "mediocre" in new areas, and that can drag the entire organization down. Some examples of the strengths of a business are listed in **Figure 5**. They can be broad-based, like decision-making ability (small and agile or big and powerful), people (strong training or good recruiting), continuity of the leadership (little turnover and a good succession plan). Strengths can be on the financial side of the business, like a good balance sheet, or they can be the products themselves, or even the product development pipeline. Strengths can even be as nebulous as a product's image, the image in the market, or even the company image overall.

Weaknesses – The Achilles heel of an organization is its weaknesses. If it does not find its important and critical weaknesses, the entire organization will be vulnerable; left unidentified and unaddressed, such weaknesses might even take the business down.

The weaknesses of an organization can be simple but devastating. The cost structure might be the only problem in the company. The wages are too high or the overhead is too high, or it might be that the overhead is just wrongly allocated. These issues sound clear and simple but they can easily cause a business to fail. The weaknesses can be very complicated and very hard to change. They may be so hard to find that even highly paid consultants cannot find the core problem. These weaknesses might be the management structure, the attitudes of the people, or even the human resource system (too simple or too bureaucratic). Some organizations can find the problems, but when they do it is often too difficult—or even too late—to change them.

Opportunities – Most organizations want to continuously improve, and most need to or the competition will start to catch up with them. This area is so important that a big part of a previous chapter was dedicated to the topic. The key opportunities of an organization are its best chance to move ahead. These opportunities need to be identified; there must be plans to develop and implement every one of them, as soon as possible. It is management's role to clear the path with mentors or sponsors and get results from these ideas.

Threats – Businesses seem to look at threats of competition as coming from the outside, from other businesses. However, some of the biggest threats come from inside an organization. Sure the competitors are a big threat—they want your customers, they don't want you to survive. A good competitor will do whatever it can to cause its competition to fail. It is very obvious that threats come from competitors, but what about the less obvious threats from the inside? The biggest threat to an organization can be hard to deal with, such as business distractions. A business might be so internally focused that it forgets what it is all about. The internal threat can be so large that it stops the business from moving ahead. The business might be focused on internal politics and forget about the outside threat(s). It may just die from the inside. Other major threats might be from the financial side of the business: it might be undercapitalized, have the wrong financial structure, or have cash flow problems. Finally, the biggest threat might be putting too many eggs in one basket by having too much business with one or a few customers, or too much of the business dependent on a few key employees.

SWOT Analysis
Figure 5

Strengths

- Quality of Products
- Professional Image

- Decision-making Ability
- People on the Team
- Market Image
- Continuity of Leadership
- Financial Stability
- Team Cares About the Business

Opportunities

- New Products
- New Product Line Extensions
- International Business
- Expand Sales Channels
- Expand Marketing
- Product Pipeline

Weaknesses

- Efficiencies

- Systems (HR, Communication, Product)
- Development Plans
- Structure

- Location

Threats

- New Competition (Present or New Companies)
- High Customer Concentration
- Business Distractions
- Suppliers (Costs & Availability)
- Inflation
- Sources of Financing

Chapter Six

PROVE THE BUSINESS CONCEPT & EXPAND ON IT

All businesses are started on a concept of success. A business that has been successful has proved that the concept works. This concept must always be challenged or the successful business might run out of steam and not be successful in the future. This chapter will help a business manager who has a new concept and wants to start a new business venture. It asks some hard questions about what makes the concept possibly work. This chapter is also valuable for the manager who wants to challenge the present business concept and reinvent—or just enhance—the business (see **Figure 6**). Finally, this chapter can be real helpful to the manager who wants to take a proven concept and expand on it.

The first step in trying to start a new business, or reinvent, enhance, or extend a pre-existing one, is to look internally at the business concept. This means a review of what makes the business or the growth of the business a valid concept. **"What is the objective of the concept review?"** This is an excellent place to start. Is the objective to start a test business or new product and see if the business works? Is the objective to review what makes the business or product line successful and develop a plan to expand on a concept that is working?

Once the objective has been determined, the business concept can be tested. There is a vision of what the business is and can be. A statement can be made that says, **"I believe that the product brand is very successful and it can be expanded for even more success."** The concept might be totally different. The belief might be that the product line needs new designs or a new sales channel. It might be that an entire revamping of the business is in order. It may also be something as simple as **"I believe that there is nothing like this new product in the market and the consumer wants this product."** The purpose of this exercise is to force a vision statement and a true passion which will drive the business now or drive it to a next or future stage.

The next business driver is to find out what the **Keys to Success** are. Up to this point, the objectives have been determined and the business has committed to its belief in a successful future state. The next goal is to find out what success would look like. Would the business and the new manager be successful if the margins increased? Would success be a whole new product line? Would success be an increase in investors? Success could even be improving the overall throughput, customer satisfaction, or operations efficiency. A broader success pattern might be necessary to look at success as an expansion of the business. The success of the business might be finding a new sales channel, having a constant pipeline of new products available, or reaching a 20% return on investment (ROI) for the investors.

The time horizon is critical in establishing the right plan. Does the business have the time to plan and implement the strategy? Is the timeline the present or is it going to take 3-5 years to see the benefits of the plan? Does the business have the time? Will the investors have the patience? Will the customers wait? When will the time run out? The customers, investors, and employees might be very patient and they may be in no hurry to get the plan implemented. All this needs to be determined at the beginning of the new business or the beginning of a change in the business.

Making a sale is really part hard work, part relationships, part product or service, part pricing, part people involved, and just a little luck. All of these elements might line up perfectly and yet, for some reason, the deal is not closed. **With no sales, there is no business**. The sales channel must be examined very carefully and changed even more carefully. One major mistake in the sales area and the business is suddenly at risk. The new manager or the management team must look into the details of **how sales are generated.** What are the elements of getting the customer to use the product or service and to pay for it? Are sales

generated through marketing and advertising? Are the sales generated
by the push sales person? Is it the product placement or pricing that
really drives sales? Several of these areas may need to be adjusted and
tested to find out the real answers to these sales questions. Is there an
element of international sales that can bring new life to an old product? How can the sales be generated best by marketing, advertising,
and promotion?

The final set of questions that need to be asked revolves around
what generates sales. These are questions at an even more basic level.
The next questions to ask have to do with how the products really sell.

There are hundreds of ways to sell a product or service. Does it take
constant calling? Does it take a long-term relationship? Does it take a
new promotion and lower price or even a giveaway? Customers can be
hard to understand. A lot of time to study the customer base is always
required to understand what causes customers to buy the product or
service. Success stories are a very good way to sell certain products.
Some customers want to know why other customers purchased the
product or service and what their success was with it. Some customers,
however, will not go for either the success story or the relationship
approach. They might want the lowest price, the least amount of hassle,
or the best quality guarantee. The key, again, is to know the product, to
know the market, and, most importantly, to know the customers and
what makes them want to buy a certain product or service.

Proof of Concept & Expand
Figure 6

	Proof of Concept Build Success	**Expand Upon Success**
Objective:	-Get wins to prove the concept	-Leverage success and take new offerings to market
What We Believe:	-Customers want new products -More sales channels lead to more sales	-Success is replicable -New products or services equals new sales -Same concepts, product extension, new sales -Same relationships, new products, new sales
Key Success Factors:	-Margin drives investment & success -Creative new products -Product quality & innovation	-Constant new products pipeline -New targeted outlets are critical -Product Promotion and internal efficiency
Timing:	-Present	-2-5 Year Horizon
How Sales Are Generated:	-Product placement -Appropriate pricing -Marketing & promotion	-Maturing products need advertising -Product visibility & promotion -International rollout
How the Products or Services Are Sold:	-Meetings with channel representatives -Persistence, relationships & constant drive	-Success stories, uniqueness, new brands -Continuous meetings with key people

Chapter Seven

FINDING THE KEY BUSINESS DRIVERS

Every business has a handful of drivers that makes the business accelerate. A new manager to the company or to the department needs to find those key drivers immediately. A key driver is the lever that a manager wants to know and influence to drive the business. If the business needs sales, what is the key driver that will increase sales? If a business needs to cut costs fast to achieve the budget or the market forecast, what can the manager do to make that goal? If the business or department needs some good news to report to its manager or the markets, where can it get good news fast? Finally, if the business needs cash or new investment, where can it get that cash or investment?

It is very difficult in some cases to find all the key levers to run the business, but it will be worth the effort to make sure that sales targets are achieved, to make sure that financial targets are met, and to ensure that the manager's support team maintains its confidence in the manager and in itself. Sometimes the key factors are easy to find but they are forgotten about and they don't get used when they are needed. The key levers are very important to find no matter how hard or easy it is to do so. An experienced manager knows where all the levers are, keeps them close to her, and knows when and when not to use them.

A good question to ask at this point is, "Why not use the levers all the time?" A manager can use the key levers all the time and continue to get an immediate, positive impact, but usually there is a price to pay. Focusing the department's or the company's resources on getting a key lever initiated can focus the company or department on short-term results at the expense of the long term. Sometimes an organization needs to pull the levers and go for the short-term result—but it must know the consequences. An example of focusing on the short term at the expense of the long term can be found in all of the key lever areas. If an organization wants immediate sales, it may ask all the sales representatives to go to their customers and get the sales for the present month. The negative consequences could be that a large future deal is put on hold or another deal must go at a lower price to get an immediate close.

Key levers usually get short-term results just as they are expected to do, but they can cause unwanted consequences and the manager must decide if it is worth it to go for the key lever and live with the consequences. A financial example of using the key lever and then living with the outcome can happen at the end of a quarter when the business needs to hit its financial target for that period. A key lever in the financial area is laying off employees and closing down production, marketing, or research departments. A department manager might be faced with the same pressure and stop the development of a good idea, hoping to get back to the development at a later date. The key lever was enacted, the financial result was achieved, but the consequence could hurt the business. The costs were reduced but some key employees could have been laid off and lost. A key project that is the foundation of future results can be shut down to help the business hit the short-term result, but that action can slow down the results of a new, important development.

Figure 7 shows how a sales key lever can be found and used to help drive the business results. Sales is usually one of the key levers for almost every organization. The objective is to find immediate, profitable sales so that the organization can achieve its sales goals. The management team in this example has decided that there are four sales channels that can be tapped to get immediate sales. The present customer base is usually a great place to find immediate, new sales. The sales representatives are asked to go to all their present customers and find new sales of the present products that they use. The sales representative might have to give a lower price or a special promotion to get the immediate sales. The next question that the sales representatives might ask their present customers is "What else can the company do?" The sales representatives might talk to their customers about new products of theirs that the customer does not use. They may bundle the present products and the new products into one package. They may have to sell more of a popular product for the customer to purchase some of the lower-selling products.

The next lever for finding immediate sales is taking the present products to a new list of customers. A good organization should have a list of potential customers ready to call on when it needs sales. The organization will probably get some new sales, but it usually takes longer to sell to new customers than to present customers. The new sales might take time away from the sales representative and his relationship with the present customers, and it could hurt long-term sales. The final example of getting immediate sales in this instance comes from rushing new products to market and selling them to new customers. The new product might be a killer product and the organization will get immediate sales, but rushing a new product to market can cause major problems if the product does not meet expectations.

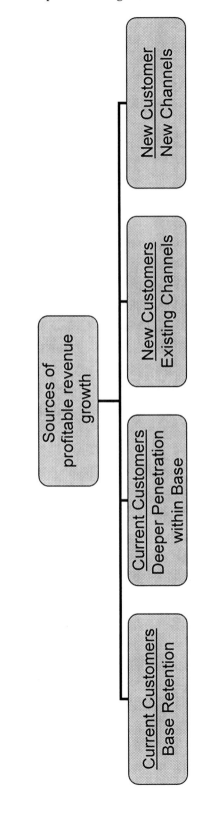

Key Drivers
Figure 7

Chapter Eight

STRUCTURE FOLLOWS STRATEGY

The typical business has a lot of pressure to optimize the individual results of each department, or even the various results inside a department. Most organizations are set up in groups, like the production department, finance department, sales department—and the list goes on. Each department is then divided up into sections within the department. The finance department can have sections like the tax department, the accounting department, the treasury department, just to name a few. The slicing up of a company helps to manage the company. Every department has goals to achieve and that helps the department manager control her environment. If a team has goals it can have control over, it is much easier for it to make a difference and control the results. This system has been successful for years, even centuries, but it can lead to sub-optimization of the company's results. The overlap of departments in the company must be managed. An example of how a company can get into this sub-optimization trap can be easily illustrated by the normal struggle between the production and the sales departments.

The production department might have a goal of reducing the overall costs of its department, so it cuts back on its staffing, or the product specifications, and achieves its goals. However, the staffing that was cut could be necessary to support the sales department's goals. The product specifications might be cut back and those specifications are required by the customer so the sales department is now faced with a tougher sale. These examples are pretty obvious but suffice for demonstration purposes; the point is, the exact same struggle happens all the time in businesses in more subtle ways. The department manager and the company leaders need to divide up their departments—and the company as a whole—to be able to manage their businesses, but they also need to tie all the pieces together to get the best overall company results.

The chart in **Figure 8** gives the manager a tool to help bring the departments together and the pieces of a department together. The chart also helps managers to get all the system inside the company to work together to get the best overall result. This process can be called "Internal Boundary Management."

What are the sales-specific questions that the company should be asking in order to think through the right sales structure and systems? The first questions can be discussed here, but further questions will be asked in more depth when other sections—like the rewards systems and the information systems—are discussed. The sales team must ask about the required sales channels, the advertising needs, the required promotional activities, the best sales organization chart, and the leadership style necessary to implement and support the company or department strategy.

Structure – There are several ways to look at the structure of the company or an individual department. The function of the department must be examined and its purpose clear; this is a good place to start. The next step is to determine the levels of authority that management desires and supports for the strategy. The questions to ask are "How many levels of management are necessary?" and "What is the decision-making authority each level should have?" Every strategy and organization will require a structure that is different and appropriate for the needs of the business. It seems that it is usually best to have as few levels as possible and to allow decision-making at the lowest level to help make the organization as responsive and flexible as possible. The simpler the organization, the better the communication. An organization will also need to decide which reward systems are appropriate to support the strategy and the amount of teamwork desired.

Staffing – Now that the structure is set up, the staffing for that structure should be examined. What kinds of skills are best for the structure? What style of organization will be helpful? What are the hiring practices desired? What does the pay structure look like? What are the human resource practices and the affirmative action policies? Who has what decision-making ability? What is the right staffing level? Too much staffing and the costs are too high. Too much staffing and the politics increase. Too little staffing and important tasks and projects do not get done. The result is too many hours, too much stress, and an increase in turnover. These questions can only be answered by the management team and the decisions should be made by the managers closest to the needs as long as they have the right skills and know the strategy.

Style – Every company has a different style. The style follows the top manager's style, the business strategy, and the business market. Some businesses need an authoritarian style since the key levers in their business are that the lowest costs win and the business does not require a lot of creativity. Some businesses require a lot of creativity and the style of management may best be a team-based system that gets everyone involved and allows the creativity to be as fluid as possible. Some organizations are quite decentralized as their customer base is geographically spread out; their style might need to reflect this decentralization, with the manager closest to the customer making a lot of the decisions. There is no right or wrong style, only the best style for the situation, the market, and the strategy.

The culture of the organization is critical to the survival of the organization. If the culture of an organization is not examined and developed into one that is supportive to the strategy, the culture will evolve itself. The evolving culture might not be a good one for the organization and might not support the strategy. The culture is the combination of activities and decisions that happen in an organization. It includes the way people act under certain conditions and how the organization responds to circumstances. For example, the culture might be to constantly avoid conflict and make decisions very slowly and methodically. This style might work well for organizations that move slowly in a slowly changing market. The organization might be in an environment where a bad decision can devastate it; the culture, in this case, might be appropriate, but would not work in a market which changes frequently and fast.

Systems – The last step in developing an organization that supports the strategy and the structure is developing the systems that make the strategy and structure work. The overview of the systems might also be for individual departments that are new or even for departments or companies that have been in existence for many years but need a review. The most obvious systems an organization needs are the information systems or the computer systems. A business manager is like the captain of a large ship. The manager must have the best possible information to steer that ship. A business manager who does not have good information or a good knowledge of the key levers is like a captain on a ship that does not have a navigation system or control of the rudder. The company and the department need to have systems to achieve their strategy. The organization must have communications systems (how do customers and employees know what is going on in the organization?). The organization must have pay systems to support the strategy. There are requirements for the development system of the employees and the development of the business systems. There are also systems that are specific to organizations for a defined market. A brainstorming session with people involved in the market and the business will quickly generate all the systems necessary for the business to achieve its strategy.

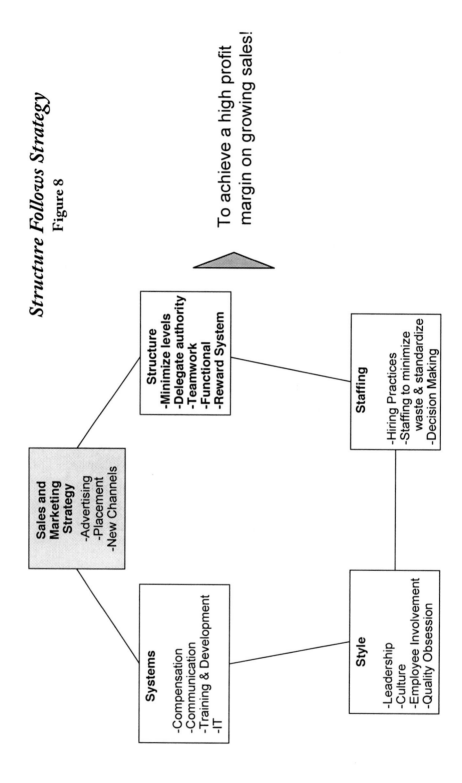

Structure Follows Strategy
Figure 8

To achieve a high profit margin on growing sales!

Sales and Marketing Strategy
-Advertising
-Placement
-New Channels

Structure
-Minimize levels
-Delegate authority
-Teamwork
-Functional
-Reward System

Staffing
-Hiring Practices
-Staffing to minimize waste & standardize
-Decision Making

Systems
-Compensation
-Communication
-Training & Development
-IT

Style
-Leadership
-Culture
-Employee Involvement
-Quality Obsession

Chapter Nine

DEVELOPING A VALUE PROPOSITION

The value proposition is part of the strategy development process. Every business or organization has a unique value to the market or there would be no reason for that business or organization to exist. Many businesses know what their reason for existence is when they start up but over time lose their way and forget about what had made them great. Many organizations change over time—or the market they serve changes over time—and can lose track of why they are in business. Sometimes the market changes and they are not able to meet its new demands. Developing or updating the value proposition will help the organization understand its unique value to the market and make clear to everyone why it is in business.

The Value Proposition is a statement that clarifies why an organization is in business or why it is a viable entity. There may be one thing that sets a business apart from the competition or there may be several things that set it apart. Most people who work in a business have an idea why they are successful but they may not know the entire reason. Sometimes people think that their department is the reason that the business is successful, but it may be the farthest thing from the truth. A department might think it is special and that false premise might cause the overall business to be less competitive. For example, a production department might think that it is the main reason for the company's success and so it does not worry about improving. The truth might be that the value proposition is the research and development department and their new products. In this example, the production department is already too costly and their lack of continuous improvement causes even more of a financial burden on the company. They must know the truth.

There are probably at least a couple of value propositions in a successful company. Identifying those value propositions will really help the internal organization to understand what is special about the company. Understanding the real value should drive the company to find even more value propositions. The largest benefit of developing the value proposition may come from outside the organization. The sales force will find that a clear and concise value proposition will make it easier to talk to the customer about the company's competitive advantages and its features and benefits. The investors and potential investors will also want to know why they should invest in this company.

The successful company clearly benefits from going through the exercise of developing its value propositions. The struggling company will gain even more from developing at least one value proposition. A struggling company might be in that position because it did not change with the market or because it forgot why it was in business. Some companies were purchased by or merged with another company and there is a new reason for their existence. The manager of a struggling company or a struggling department needs to develop a new strategy. Part of developing that new strategy is looking internally and finding out what makes that company special or unique and why the customers should consider them for business.

The chart in **Figure 9** will help the successful and struggling company alike to develop a value proposition. The chart looks at three potential value propositions across the top and five potential characteristics of the value proposition with the heading for each on the left hand side. The following descriptions go through each of those five characteristics and give examples for each of the three potential value propositions.

Potential Value Propositions – The chart outlines three potential value propositions. They are Operational Excellence, Product Leadership, and Customer Intimacy. The concept, in this example, is that the organization is really good at these three areas. The operation is probably a low cost provider in the markets it serves. The products that come from the research & development or product development departments are the leaders in the industry. The sales, marketing, and customer service departments have developed a strong relationship with the customers. They know the customers and their businesses so well that there is an unusual and strongly positive bond. These three potential value propositions Drive Better Value to the customers.

1) **Value Proposition Benefits** – The operational excellence of the company drives the lowest cost structure for itself and its customers. Product leadership drives the best product designs and the best product quality for the customers. The customer intimacy drives the best customer response with the shortest response time.

2) **Golden Rule** – A golden rule for the operational excellence team could be to eliminate waste. A golden rule for the product development team might be to build on a successful product line, innovate, and always be open to new ideas.

3) **Core Processes** – The key to a value proposition is that a certain department or process in the company is special at delivering value to the customer. The operational excellence core process could be the production design, the distribution process, or the order processing system. The product leadership core processes could be innovation, creativity, or even market exploitation. The customer intimacy core processes might be retailer or customer contacts, constant communication, or a special advertising style.

4) **Organization and Culture** – The organizational style and the culture of an operational excellence value proposition might be simplification, waste elimination, and standardization of processes. The product leadership organization might be set up to have a fluid and flexible structure and a culture of reduced R&D cycle times, with strong decision-making and some tolerance for risk. An organization that has a special intimacy with its customers might be organized for decentralized decisions. The company representative that is closest to the customer has the authority to make the right decisions to take care of the customer. This organization will probably be both customer- and field-driven.

5) **Improvement Levers** – An organization usually has some levers that can be pulled to improve results. This concept was discussed in an earlier chapter. The operational excellence levers might be the just-in-time delivery system. The operational excellence organization will always be looking for operational or process improvements. A new change here can really help the organization and the customer. A new supplier's cost reduction or process improvement will make a large difference in the costs of doing business and/or the price to the customer.

The product leadership team might find a new supply or supplier that improves the products. The customers will benefit almost immediately. A reduced R&D cycle can bring a new product to market faster and just in time to help the company and the customer. An organization that is really good at customer intimacy might be able to leverage that relationship with expertise that helps the customer, and that could bring in new sales. The organization might be able to take more risks because it knows that the strong intimacy with the customer will help it through any potential problems. The key levers in this area always revolve around the customer. An organization that has a value proposition of customer intimacy always focuses on the customer's needs.

Value Propositions

Figure 9

Example

Driving Better Value

	Operational Excellence	Product Leadership	Customer Intimacy
Value Propositions	• Best Total Cost	• Best Designs • Best Product Quality	• Best Customer Response
Golden Rule	• Eliminate Waste	• Replicate Success • Innovate • Open to Imagination	• Analyze Reactions (Customer & Store)
Core Processes	• Designs • Order Processing • Distribution	• Invention • Creativity • Market Exploitation	• Retailer Contact • Communication • Advertising
Organization and Culture	• Simplification • Waste Elimination	• Standardized Procedures	
Improvement Levers	• Just-in-time Supplies	• Process Improvements • Reduce Supplies Costs	

Chapter Ten

COMPETITIVE ANALYSIS

The company strategy is not complete without a review of the competitors in the market. Companies want all of their competition to go away or at least not compete as hard. In the present world, most businesses have a lot of competition and they must compete daily. If competitors can make business difficult for everyone else in their market, they will usually be more successful. A strong analysis of what the competitors are doing, with a comparison and a contrast of all companies' strengths and weaknesses, will help the strategy development. The focus will then be on the critical elements of the strategy. A good tool to help the company analyze what is important and how it competes is found in **Figure 10.**

The chart titled "Competitive Analysis" is found in **Figure 10.** This chart does not attempt to answer all of the issues related to the competition but is focused on setting the framework for the strategic plan. The competitive analysis fits the competition into this framework for further analysis. There are several key attributes that need to be analyzed and measured against the competition. These are the key areas where a competitor can make it difficult for the company's managers. The key areas are where they compete against other such as **sales & marketing, price, and market share.** Certain companies that have unique products or services need to also focus on the products or services that they have in the market. The analysis needs to look into how their **products and services** stack up against the competition.

Analyzing the competition should look at what is important in the market and how the company and its products and services compare against the competition. This first step should be an overview and then the details can be examined more closely. The matrix in **Figure 10** will help the company management or a department's management figure out what is important to them and what they should focus on. The top of the chart shows the relative weighting for each column. The columns move from **Weaknesses** in the company to the **Strengths** in the company. The scale on the left hand side of the chart weights the relative importance of key aspects in the market from the top, which is high importance, to the bottom of the scale, which is relatively unimportant. All key competitive elements of the market and the relative comparison to the competitors can be charted on this matrix.

A few examples of what to evaluate and how to evaluate the company's relative position to the competitor will illustrate the usefulness of the chart. This exercise is really a compare and contrast exercise between the company and its competition in the marketplace. There are several areas that the compare and contrast can be focused on but the following list will help the new manager and even the experienced manager get started. The analysis starts with the general placement of an attribute on the chart but then it discusses the situation in a little more detail.

Competitive Analysis (example)

1) **Financial Strength** – The financial strength of the company is of high importance since it is critical to the product development strategy, its investment strategy, and its advertising and marketing strategy. The company in this example does not have a very good balance sheet and could not withstand a severe or long-term drop in the market. Relatively speaking, the company is not in a very good financial position in comparison to its competitors, so it could not withstand a drop in prices or a product development battle with the competition. The company needs to keep this very important element in mind when it is finalizing its strategy.

2) **Economy of Scale** – The company in this example is a medium-size company so its economy of scale is fairly high compared to the many small companies in this industry. However, it scores low compared to the large companies that dominate the market. Economy

of scale is very important in this industry because it lets the larger companies buy their supplies at a much lower price. This company scored low on the rating scale in this important category. This says that the company could get into price wars with the smaller companies but not with the larger ones.

3) **Distribution Costs** – The location and the size of a company can have a major impact on the costs to distribute their products. A company that is in a central location can service far more of the entire market and meet faster product delivery timelines. This category may be really important to some companies but not to others. A company might not worry about distribution costs if it is small and very close to the customer; in fact, this positioning might be just the advantage that a smaller company needs. The example in the chart shows a company that scores low in a low importance category, so there is little to worry about in this area.

4) **Pricing** – One of the most important categories to score well in is the pricing of the product. The first step is to analyze the company's position and then decide if there is a problem. This company is at about parity with its competitors on price because its cost structure is about average. It does not have a product that can demand a higher than average price. This is not a competitive advantage that can help the company get ahead.

5) **Quality** – The company in this example is very strong in the quality area. The products are priced at about average but they give more value to the customer than anyone else in the market. In the industry it is in this is a very important category, and it is one of the core competencies of the company. The strategic plan for this company should clearly utilize this important advantage in the market with its sales force and customers. Advertising and promotional campaigns need to highlight the quality advantage.

6) **Product Design** – Product design is very important in many industries and especially important to this company and this industry. The product design probably leads to the high quality attributes that this company possesses. The product design department should continue to get the funding that it needs to stay ahead of the competition. Cutting the funding of the design department might save

money in the short term but hurt the company in one of the only competitive advantages that it has.

7) **Customer Service** – This company does not need an excellent customer service department because the products don't require it. The industry typically does not fully utilize a customer service department. The company is scoring very high on a service that may not need to be funded at a high level. The company is probably over-funding its customer service department and can better and more appropriately use those very valuable resources in another department.

Competitive Analysis
Figure 10

	Weakness	Parity	Strength
Versus Main Competitors			
High Importance	-Financial Strength		-Quality -Product Designs -Ease of Use
	-Economy of Scale		
	-Market Awareness	-Pricing	-Customer Service
		-Customer Relationships	
Competitive Value	-Distribution Costs		
Low Importance	-Vertically Integrated		-First to Market
	Low Rating	Competitive Score	High Rating

Chapter Eleven

RESPONSIBILITY CHARTING

The business manager has developed a good plan to build or rebuild the business. The plan is probably for a department but it could be for the entire business. This plan has many key elements included. It probably focuses on several key elements of the business, such as the people development, the finances of the department or company, the budget, sales, marketing, the advertising campaign, product development, etc. The plan needs to be detail-focused to ensure that all the key elements of the plan get implemented. The manager now needs a tool to help him implement the strategy and ensure that everything gets done. A plan is only as good as the details that get done and done well. Most organizations have a tool to help in project management or project implementation. The chart in **Figure 11** is listed as a recommendation if the organization does not have a standard for project management or the team is looking for a new tool.

Responsibility Charting is simply a tool for project management. The key elements of a plan are listed. The priority of each is analyzed and noted. The leader of each action step is documented and then reasonable implementation dates are listed. If the action is complicated and time-consuming, interim implementation dates are listed with a note added. The attached chart in **Figure 11** is simple but very effective. If everyone who has the responsibility to implement an action step is given a copy of the chart, and they have a chance to decide on the dates, they are very likely to achieve the goals they are supposed to implement. All key managers should get a copy of the responsibility chart. The chart in **Figure 11** is easy to set up and use but a brief description of the chart will eliminate any potential for confusion or misunderstanding.

1) **Functional Area** – There are typically several functional areas in a business, such as: operations, finance, sales and marketing, human resources, and research & development. Every one of these major areas is broken down into 5, 6, or 7 functional areas with a more specific focus. For example, finance is broken into accounting, purchasing, accounts payable, collections, taxes, etc. It is important to highlight which area of the company or department will follow up on the action step to ensure that the responsibility for implementation and change is not concentrated in only one department. It is also key to seeing which parts of the company or department need the most change.

2) **Description** – This section is a short description of what the project is really about. An example is the finance functional area project, which is to "Refinance the Bank Loan." The company may need a more competitive rate, or relief from a certain bank covenant, or a longer period of time to pay off the loan. The description should list the objective of the loan refinancing, such as "spread the payments over a few more years to lower the monthly payment by X%." This example describes a very clear action step with which the leader can implement the task.

3) **Leader** – This column indicates who has the ultimate responsibility to implement the action step listed in the description area. In the example above, the CFO is the ultimate person to make sure the action steps get implemented and that the result meets the criteria. The CFO might delegate the responsibility to another person on the team, but the CFO is ultimately responsible and needs to report progress in the management meetings.

4) **Support** – Very few projects can be implemented successfully by one person or a small team. Usually the entire company or department must support the implementation of high level and critical projects. The support needed might be other team members' time, or just their verbal support. The CFO in this example might need some cash to buy down the loan's interest rate. The CFO might need the CEO's support to review and sign the documents. The

CFO might need a lawyer's review of the documents. Many times capital is required to implement the appropriate action steps.

5) **Due Date, Priority, and Notes** – These final three columns are much easier to describe but still important. In the example above, the entire team depends on the CFO to get a new and appropriate loan completed in order to achieve success. Sometimes other action steps cannot be accomplished until this action step is completed, which should be done as soon as possible. The priority setting is also very important. The top priorities will get the first look and the most attention. The priorities should be evenly distributed. There should be only about 5 levels of priority set up to help management focus on the most important goals. It is always a good idea to take notes on all key action items.

Responsibility Charting
Figure 11

Functional Area	Description
Leadership	Senior Management Strategic Planning
Production	Competitive Bidding
Banking	Refinance Loan
Sales	International Sales Plans
Sales	Complete NewProduct Rollout
Sales/Operations	New Product Customer Service Support System
Communication	Monthly Meetings with Team
Sales	Reintroduce Old Products that Need Support
Operations	Review All Internal Processes
Human Resources	Develop a NewPay System
Human Resources	Develop an Evaluation System
Human Resources	Set Up a Skills Development Program
Marketing	Develop a Marketing & Promotion Plan
Design	Develop a Core Product Pipeline
Design	Develop a NewProduct Development Process
Operations	Review all Suppliers Agreements & Costs
Marketing	Detailed Competitive Analysis Review

Leader	Support	Due Date	Printing	Notes
	Management Team	2/1/2006	1	
COO	VP Sales	3/1/2006	1	
CFO	CEO	3/1/2006	1	
VP Sales	COO	3/1/2006	1	
VP Sales	COO	4/1/2006	1	
VP Sales	COO	5/1/2006	2	
VP HR	CEO	3/1/2006	2	
VP Sales	Customer Service	5/1/2006	2	
COO	CFO	4/1/2006	2	
VP HR	COO	5/1/2006	3	
VP HR	COO	5/1/2006	3	
VP HR	COO	7/1/2006	3	
VP Sales	CEO	5/1/2006	2	
Research Director	Design Team	5/1/2006	2	
Research Director	Design Team	6/1/2006	3	
COO	Purchasing	7/1/2006	3	
VP Sales	Management Team	8/1/2006	3	

Chapter Twelve

STRATEGIC TAKEAWAYS

The Strategy is probably developed by this stage in the building process. The 3-year financial plan has probably developed and the yearly budget is in place. (There are many books available to help the company or department develop their financial plans after the strategy has been developed. These details are not covered here.) The tracking system has been set up through Responsibility Charting to ensure that the plan is implemented. Now all of the stakeholders need a summary of the goals and plans to help them see the broader picture. The overview will also give the key participants a document for discussion. A one-page **Strategic Takeaway** list will help management to show the employees, shareholders, vendors, etc., what the essence of the strategic plan entails and what their responsibilities are within it.

The chart in **Figure 12** will help management convey the key messages to the organization on what is important. The chart also shows what parts of the business will change over the next year or years. The strategic takeaways list should incorporate most if not all of the actions in the responsibility chart. In this example list, the strategic takeaways are an attempt to summarize the Strategic Plan and the details of the Responsibility Chart. The **Goal** of this example is to position the company or department for short-term and long-term success. There are statements in the strategy for everyone in these major company initiatives. A short description of each of these strategic statements is listed below. This will help all stakeholders know the plan and be able to discuss it succinctly.

1) This statement tells everyone that efficiency, advertising, business focus, and cost cutting are critical because the business is maturing and these actions must be implemented.

2) This statement implies that the domestic market is maturing and the international market is one of the best next opportunities for growth.

3) The product or service life cycles are slowing down and new products must be developed for the company to remain financially healthy.

4) Growth has been fairly easy in the past and did not need a detailed strategy or plan. However, this statement warns that, in the future, growth will be harder to achieve, and a plan with clear action steps will now be required.

5) The need for creativity and new, out-of-the-box thinking is now even more critical for this company. The management team must express the need for new ideas. The philosophy of the company is to achieve new, out-of-the-box ideas through the employees. The concept of employee involvement will help initiate these ideas.

6) Obsession with quality has always been a key to the company's success in this example. The management team wants it to be clear that quality is even more critical now than it has always been. The second message the management team wants to make clear is that obsession with high quality must be the passion of every person in the company in order for this company to achieve its goals.

There are several different ways a company's strategy can be communicated. There are several areas that strategic statements can emphasize. The key for management is to publish a list of summarized strategic statements to all stakeholders so all essential people understand the essence of the Strategy!

Strategic Takeaways
Figure 12

Goal - To be positioned well for success in the current year and beyond

1) The core business is maturing and this means efficienc y, advertising, a clear business focus, and a cost-cutting culture are critical

2) International business is a major new opportunity

3) New products or services are the key to the future

4) Future growth will now need a plan with an implementation strategy

5) Employee involvement with a culture that encourages participation and out-of the-box thinking is critical

6) Obsession with product quality & innovation must permeate the entire team

AN EMPLOYEE DEVELOPMENT PROCESS

The Employee Development Guide is intended to be just what its title implies—a guide to employee development activities. It is not intended to spell out rigid rules of administration.

Employee development is a key responsibility of each manager. As this guide points out, each manager shares that responsibility with her own manager. Effective development, then, is a joint effort between each manager and employee. As such, it requires ongoing formal and informal activities, discussion and dialogue, planning and execution. Effective development has the characteristic of being "tailored" for each individual, based on that individual's development needs and career desires.

This guide sets forth the "formal activity" portion of development. These activities should be carried out as a part of each employee's development program. The method used may vary but the full intent of each activity should be met. For example, the method used to develop and present results expectations may be different, but it is the intent that all employees have a set of written, comprehensive results expectations.

The guide should help each employee understand and monitor his own development activities and how they mesh together into a total development program. This understanding should promote more meaningful discussion between managers and employees.

The process will also serve as a training guide for managers. It should be used to help make each manager a more effective developer of her employees.

Chapter One

DEVELOPING A PLAN

Developing people is similar, in many ways, to developing a business. A business needs constant attention and development with a continuous improvement process. People need the same attention and development. All continuous improvement endeavors—including employee development—rely on a process to make the development as efficient and effective as possible. The purpose of this chapter is to outline a proven process for the development of people in a business environment.

There are three main blocks in this development process and they are outlined in detail in **Figure 1**. (All of the Development Blocks and Action Steps are described in detail in the following chapters). The first training block in the continuous development of people is planning the process; the second block is the actual development process; and the final block is measuring the result of the process. Since this process is the continuous development of people, the process goes through a set of continuous development steps and then starts over again. Then it goes through the process again, and again—probably once per year, every year. The more this process is used, the more opportunities for development the employees will receive.

The following steps usually are included in block one, the Planning Process:

- **Step One** – The first step should be a joint expectation-sharing including the manager and the employee.

- **Step Two** – The next step is defining the job expectations in detail and then writing a job description based on the shared expectation.

- **Step Three** – The final step in the planning process is the clear communication of the expectations, the job definition, and the detailed job description.

Block two focuses on the Development Process in the following steps:

- **Step One** – It is crucial to observe the employee's actions and "inspect what you expect."

- **Step Two** – Employees deserve to hear the elements of the managers' observations as soon as possible. An employee should not have to wait until the annual performance appraisal to find out how he can improve.

- **Step Three** – This is the beginning of the continuous improvement process. After the employee hears the feedback from the manager's first observations, he and the manager should write a short improvement plan. This should be a continual process. Every time a manager sees a major need for employee development, the manager needs to talk to him in a coaching manner. A continuous improvement development process continues to help the employee grow.

The final development block is the Measurement block as summarized below:

- **Step One** – Perform an annual performance appraisal.

- **Step Two** – Get a second level review and signoff of the employees' performance appraisal. This second level review ensures the consistency and calibration of the reviews.

- **Step Three** – The final step of the development process is to write a detailed improvement plan which includes the top three skills and the top three needs improvements with action plans. This is the final step of the employee continuous improvement process. The path to excellence has just started. People are capable of continual growth.

Overview of the Process

Figure 1

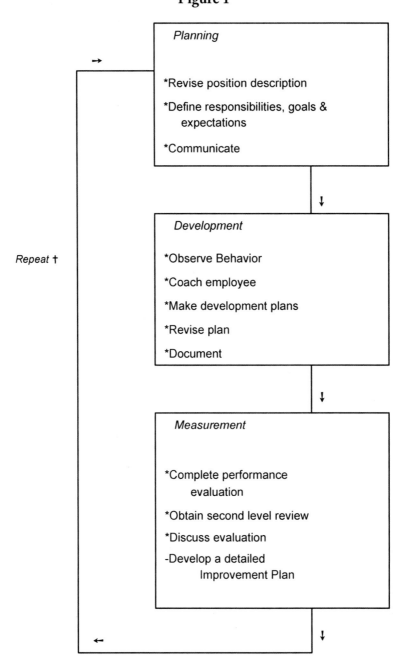

- The ability to conduct successful performance evaluations is dependant upon what has been going on all year.

Chapter Two

MANAGING BY PRINCIPLES
& NOT RULES

Many organizations, businesses, and teams develop a list of employee rules or policies. Rules are probably a good idea in many circumstances, especially sporting events where they are necessary for an equal playing field. However, this might not be the right direction in a complex business environment. The more complex the business environment, the more potential options will surface and the more variety of options people will be faced with. The more an organization tries to regulate itself in this kind of situation, the longer the list of rules to cover all the potential options. There are some organizations that manage by rules, and many do it well and are very successful. Some organizations have pages and pages of rules and can really get slowed down in their decision-making with so many different options and situations to choose from. This problem can really be exasperating in an organization that thrives on creativity. An organization can spend more time on rule-following than on developing a new product.

There are other ways to manage an organization than to build the next set of rules. There are several organizations, especially creative-based ones, switching to a principle-based set-up. An organization that lives on principles is more fluid, makes decisions faster, and usually knows what to do no matter what they face. A principle-based organization develops a list of 15-20 principles to live by such as "Every team member has something to contribute." These twenty or so principles then guide an organization and its people on what is important and how to make decisions. It is still critical to have a few rules for items that are non-negotiable and will probably never change—like zero tolerance for theft in the workplace, making stealing an immediate, terminal offence. Other than these few golden rules, the rest of the decisions a manager or team needs to make can be based on the principles of the organization.

Developing principles for an organization may sound easy to do, and it can be. The hard part is the soul-searching that will be required to find the 15-20 principles that really state what the organization stands for. These principles of leadership will be what people will live by at work.

The first step in developing principles for managing an organization is to assemble the people chosen to come up with these principles. Some organizations take just the 5-6 key leaders offsite, and spend a couple of hours brainstorming; others get the entire team together and develop them. It is very common to get as many people together as possible since the more input at the beginning the more potential for acceptance later on during implementation.

The process in developing the **Business Principles** in **Figure 2** is simple:

Step One – Assemble the right people, usually as many as possible.

Step Two – Ask everyone in the meeting to write down the one way of doing business that is really important to them. Then ask them to write down one thing they really don't like that happens in the business environment.

Step Three – Answer and clarify questions. Give out some examples that have been prepared ahead of time, or ask a couple of people to volunteer suggestions.

Step Four – Once the team is clear on the assignment, have the facilitator collect the items that people like in the business environment and then the items that they do not like in a separate group.

Step Five – Tell the group to take a break or have everyone work on another project while the items are tabulated.

Step Six – Put the items that the team liked on a flip chart. Group like items together. Try to write all items in an action-orientated statement like "We do everything efficiently the first time."

Step Seven – Check the negative items collected and compare them with the list that was just generated; see if any new ideas for the principle list arise.

Step Eight – This is the final step. The team needs to finalize the list to no more than 20 principles to make sure it is manageable—easy to remember and to live by. Some teams vote on the list and some work on them until a consensus is achieved. A little work may be required to get the exact wording that helps the team get excited enough to follow these new principles. The main work is now done.

The final result is a clear and energizing list of Business Principles to live by at work and a guide to decision-making!

Business Principles
Figure 2

Example

- Every team member has something to contribute.
- A creative, open environment is the key to success.
- Employees see a career, not just a job.
- Even one injury means failure.
- We do everything efficiently the first time.
- Teamwork and high productivity lead to financial success.
- Consistent communication leads to a strong team.
- A pipeline of new products is critical.
- Personal integrity is the foundation of business success.
- Financial stability is good for everyone.
- Our products are the best in the business.

Chapter Three

DEVELOPMENT CHECKLIST

The goal of this section of the book is the continuous development of people at work and of the business as a whole. That goal is clear; it is also clear that a process with a built-in timeline is required to make it happen. The purpose of this chapter is to implement this goal and to outline the overall process of the ongoing development of business employees. The chart in **Figure 3** takes this development and puts it into steps with timelines and dates. This chart shows some specific actions that are the key to developing people and also attaches a time-line with a section to document when an action step is completed.

The chart in **Figure 3** lists the key steps in the employee development process, described in detail below. The key to making this chart work is to go through each step and list the date that the action step should be completed. There is an area in the middle of the chart for any notes or comments. The last column is set up to track and monitor the committed dates; this ensures that all steps are completed. If the actions are not completed there needs to be documentation of why the correct actions were not done on time.

The following describes all of the action steps in the **Figure 3** chart:

- **Assignment Selection** – The continuous improvement process starts with selecting the right position for employees so that they can be successful and the company gets what it is paying for. This is an important first step and it needs to be completed on a timely basis. (This step may not be necessary if a person is going to go through the development process in the job he is currently in. If this is true—the employee will be staying in place—then the first two steps can be skipped.)

- **Department Preparation** – Once a person has been assigned to a position, the department needs to prepare for her to make sure she has the appropriate work space and tools to be successful.

- **Training Preparation** – All of the training material for a new or present employee needs to be assembled ahead of time, such as the company job requirements and the benefits program. All of these key training materials should be prepared before an employee is brought on board.

- **On Boarding** – In order for a new employee to feel comfortable and be as efficient as possible as quickly as possible, he needs to be brought on board professionally. This means getting him to his workplace and setting up a meeting with the people he will be working with.

- **Skills Assessment** – An employee needs to go though an assessment process to find out what her strengths and weaknesses are before she can begin the continuous improvement process. An employee needs to know her skills very early in the process so that she can focus on improving the key areas that will help her grow as quickly as possible.

- **Expectation Sharing** – The first major step in developing an employee is to share clear expectations with him both about his specific job and the general work environment. There are several keys to sharing expectations that will be discussed in future chapters.

- **Job Definition** – Everyone should have a job definition or job description. This is a fairly easy process, but it is amazing how many jobs don't have one. The lack of a job description can lead to an employee not knowing exactly what her job really is.

- **Goals Package** – At this stage the employee knows what his job is and what the expectations are. The next key step is to plan his goals for the next year. An employee should have 3-5 goals that are designed to make an impact on the business. He might also have 3 goals for improving his skills over the next year.

- **Feedback Sessions** – Some organizations only give feedback to employees once a year at the most—and some never. It seems to work much better not to wait until the official performance appraisal to give performance feedback. An employee may need the feedback throughout the year so that she can continually adjust and constantly improve. It is recommended that an employee get feedback at least once a quarter. It does not need to be a formal feedback session; a private coaching session will work.

- **Performance Appraisal** – Most employees know what a performance appraisal is since most companies use them. However, most companies use them as discreet events that happen once per year. There is little or no real development after it is conducted. A performance appraisal is exactly as the words state: an appraisal of the employee's performance over the specified timeframe—usually a year.

- **Problem Solving and Time Management Training** – This section can list specific training that employees can and should go through, in general, so they can grow and contribute even more to the company's results. There are a couple of examples of general training that many new and experienced employees really need. A company can compare the training needed and maybe even give training like problem solving or time management to several employees at once.

- **Career Planning** – The final step in the development process is career planning. Most employees want to have a career and not just a job. It is much easier to get an employee involved in the development process if she realizes that her development is good for the company and good for her. If she knows that the actions she is taking could lead to a better career, she will probably put more energy into the entire process.

DEVELOPMENT CHECKLIST
Figure 3

Date_____   Manager_____

Employee_____

EVENT	TARGET DATE	COMMENTS/ PLANS/ TRAINING RESOURCE NEEDS/ CONSULTING	DATE DONE
Assignment Section			
Department Preparation			
Training Preparation			
On Boarding			
Skills Assessment			
Position Expectations			
Job Definition			
Goals Package			
Feedback Sessions			
Performance Appraisal			
Time Management Training			
Problem Solving Training			
Career Planning			

Chapter Four

SETTING GENERAL EXPECTATIONS

Managers can get very frustrated with employees when they do not do what the managers were expecting. The first question a manager should ask is not "What is wrong with that employee?" but, maybe, "Was I clear with what I was expecting?" Most of the time it is the manager's fault that an expectation was not met. Employees want to do a good job in most cases, and they want to meet the manager's expectations, but many times they really don't understand what is expected of them. There are two levels of expectations in the work place: 1) the general expectations of working with the team, and 2) the job expectation, i.e., how to do the specific job and all of its requirements. The purpose of this chapter is to develop a format for what is expected in the work environment. It is key that employees know what they need to achieve in order to fit into the culture of their work group. If you are a new manager, or you have just taken over a new area of responsibility, this is a very good way to start getting your expectations clear. If you are trying to develop a work culture that you think will achieve the desired results then start by making clear what your General Expectations are.

The list of expectations of an employee could be a mile long, but that level of detail is not necessary and could even be counterproductive. Your employees are usually pretty smart and they are motivated to do what you want them to do. Think about what really is important to you and set the tone with some general guidelines on the key expectations. They will understand the expectations and follow them. If you try to cover every expectation, the list will be too long. The manager can get the employees to follow the rules and not think about what is necessary, but he needs to get them to meet the general expectations *and* to think and do the right things.

General Expectations can follow many formats, but **Figure 4** gives the manager a place to start. The general expectations are outlined in three categories: Communication, Professionalism, and Development. These three categories were specifically chosen and have been used in many organizations over several years with similar results. Employees instantly understand some of the key expectations that a manager has. They know that it is very important to communicate; they understand what professionalism is; and they understand that for the organization to constantly grow people development is critical.

Using the style and detail of **Figure 4** will give the manager a good place to start communicating expectations. This figure discusses only these three general areas of expectations and there are many more that may be important. Begin with these, and build on them at a later date, being careful not to get too specific or too lengthy. The key here—especially for a new manager—is to get an early start with employees. Employees will understand if the expectations change over time, but it is important to give them some direction at the very beginning of a new assignment as their manager. The following describes **Figure 4** in a little more detail so the new manager can get started instantly.

Communication – There is never enough communication in an organization. Sometimes there is a lot of discussion but there is always a need to communicate more. Take a survey of the employees and they will almost always say that one of the top five needs in the organization is to improve communication. Start with communication as one of your top priorities and get the employees' attention right away. Communication is important to employees and they will be very pleased to hear that it is also important to you. The expectations listed in **Figure 4** are trying to set the tone of the communication that the manager wants. It says that you want open and honest communication. It says that you want it frequently. It also says that you want to have positive and negative feedback to happen on a regular basis and not just once or twice a year. Meetings are one of the key ways to communicate and they should be efficient and well-managed. A clear expectation should be set on how important meetings are, but it also needs to be clear that they should be efficient. These actions will help employees understand your meeting expectations.

Professionalism – Every organization has a culture. Some cultures are purposefully developed but some just happen over time and by accident. The manager probably wants the organization to develop a culture that makes sense and is developed purposefully. Therefore, it is important to develop the culture rather than to let it just take shape. If the manager wants to try and shape the foundation of the culture he is leading, he should start with some expectations. The example in **Figure 4** attempts to set the tone of a culture of professionalism. It tries to define what is meant by professionalism and show some of the ways to be professional. Professionalism in this example means doing everything well, like making commitments and honoring them. It says a professional takes risks and follows through (See **Figure 4** for details). A manager can add to or subtract from these expectations on professionalism. He can look at areas other than professionalism to set the tone of the culture. But if he doesn't try to shape the culture, one will naturally evolve—and it may be one he does not like.

Development – The essence of this book is the development of the team and the development of the business. Setting general expectations on development will help build a culture that is centered on continuous improvement and a commitment to ongoing development. A manager might be expected to be an Instant Manager through a promotion or a new job. However, the exceptional manager must realize that she will have long-term success not with instant techniques and strategies but through continuous growth and development of the people and the business. The focus on development will surely get the attention of the people managed. It clearly says the manager cares enough to invest in the employees and in the business. The example in **Figure 4** talks about some of those key elements of development. It asks the team to be responsible for its own growth. It says that the managers are there to help and will be engaged in the development process but that the employees need to make sure it happens; their futures will be the ones affected, for better or worse. Finally, this figure discusses how important it is to utilize all the resources available to the employees in their development. It says: 1) use your manager in your development; 2) use all the people on the team no matter what their backgrounds are; and 3) use all their internal senses—especially their feelings and instincts—to find out how they can grow and make their development a reality.

General Expectations
Figure 4

COMMUNICATION

- Communication is vital—straight, honest, and efficient. Information should go to the appropriate people.
- Over-communication is better than under-communication.
- Feedback should be regular, ongoing, and timely. Positive and negative constructive feedback is required.
- Attendance required at Scheduled Department Meeting. Be on time; if you can't make it, let the right people know.

PROFESSIONALISM:

- Make commitments and follow through.
- Be organized and prepared for meetings and presentations.
- Know your job responsibilities.
- Say "NO" when you're overloaded.
- Provide job updates.
- Write one page monthly letters.
- Pay attention to the process as well as content.
- Manage your time.
- Involve people in your work.
- Be available as a resource.
- Be willing to take risks and make mistakes.
- Treat employees fairly and consistently.
- Recognize good employees.
- Confront poor performers and employees with other problems. Files must be well documented!

- Treat each person as an individual. Listen and respond to his/her questions, requests for information.
- Never say "Let me get back to you," if you don't intend to do it.
- Develop people through coaching, one-to-ones, feedback, questioning, critique, discipline, etc.

DEVELOPMENT:

- Be responsible for your own development.
- Don't be a "YES" person.
- Share feelings.
- Work to understand and value differences.
- Use your manager to get what you need.
- Promote from within whenever possible.

Chapter Five

SETTING JOB EXPECTATIONS

Every employee needs to have a job description. A job description is usually a written list of the expectations a manager has of the employee. Most job descriptions are written from an expectation sharing session between the two. The job description cannot cover every responsibility of the employee in every situation; it needs to cover as much detail as possible but not be more than a couple of pages. Every job description should have captions at the bottom of it, stating: "This job definition covers the major aspects of the work required, but an employee is expected to cover other activities as requested by management."

The expectation sharing session can be guided by the expectation questions in **Figure 5**. These are intended to stimulate a conversation between the manager and the employee rather than to be filled out in complete detail. The manager should take notes from the conversation and then take the information gained and write the job description. The questionnaire lists questions about the job and its expectations in three areas: Detailed Expectations of the Role and Responsibilities, Expectations of the Job, and Interpersonal Relationship Expectations.

Detailed Expectations of the Role and Responsibilities – These questions are focused on the overall role of the job and the detailed responsibilities of the job. The questions are in a general format but they should stimulate a conversation that develops all the answers to write a detailed Job Description.

Expectations of the Job – There are many expectations of the job and also the job environment. An employee can do the specifics of the job but still be unsuccessful because of other factors of the work environment such as not getting along with other employees or the manager. The purpose of these expectation questions is to try and sort out all the expectations of the job as a whole which includes both the details and expectations of the job itself and of the entire work environment.

Interpersonal Relationship Expectations – The goal of this section is to try and develop all the expectations of the employee working with other employees and the manager.

Job Expectation Checklist
Figure 5

<u>Detailed Roles & Responsibility Expectations</u>

What I think the overall team's roles and responsibilities are:

_____

What I think my manager's role is and what his/her responsibilities are:

_____

What I think my primary roles and job responsibilities are as an employee:

_____

What are the key common areas of responsibility:

_____

<u>Expectations of the Job</u>

What I want and expect from my manager:

_____

What I do not want or expect from my manager:

_____

What I think my manager expects from me:

_____

What I am willing to do to support the team and my manager:

_____

What I am not willing to do for the work environment:

_____

What I think the department's goals/plans for this year should be:

_____

Interpersonal Relationship Expectations

How will decisions and priorities that affect us be made?

_____

Situations I expect to be involved in or notified of:

_____

How does Coordination with others happen?

_____

In what ways will we support each other?

_____

How open and candid will we be with each other?

_____

Kinds of personal feedback and coaching the manager is expected to give:

_____

Kinds of personal feedback and coaching each person is expected to give:

_____

Kinds of feedback and coaching I do not want are:

_____

How will my performance be judged?

_____

By what means will we maintain an effective communication channel?

_____

What are the strengths and weaknesses of our organization?

_____

_____

Chapter Six

CAREER PLANNING

To help your employees reach their career potsentials, each one should be aided in producing a career development plan. When an employee reaches her potential and is very productive, she is a high contributor to the organization. Investing time in an employee and helping her design a career will have a high return. Having a career plan helps a person understand her strengths and needs improvements areas and figure out what kind of work will best match this profile. Understanding herself in this way will help her decide what her short- and long-term career goals will be.

The form in **Figure 6** will help any person to develop his or her short- and long-term career goals and develop a path to get there. The purpose of the first step, **Short-Range Interests**, is to list the employee's short-term interests. The next step is to review the list of interests and focus in on the top ones. Then he should examine Number 2, **Long-Range Interests**. Here he will focus on his long-term goals and interests in the same way he did with his short-term goals and interests: first he should list his long-term aspirations and then his long-term interests and, finally, narrow down his long-term interests and focus on his top career-long interests.

An employee's interests must be considered for his career planning, and his personal needs must also be considered. The next area to discuss is listed in the third section, **Personal Considerations**. The form in **Figure 6** has an area to be filled out on the topic of personal considerations. It is very important to discuss the impact of achieving a goal and taking on new responsibilities. A promotion or a job change has many potential rewards but it might also have some new challenges. It is usually good to identify any potential issues early so a plan can be developed to minimize them.

The final step in this process is to try and identify the next steps. The area in Question 4, **Interests in a Particular Assignment,** asks the employee to look around his organization and try and find out what kind of work he would like to do. He doesn't have to change jobs in order to help with some work he is interested in. Working on new challenges will help him achieve the next step in his career path. The organization will also benefit since the employee is now taking on new responsibilities in his present position and working hard to prepare himself for the next position in his career plan.

Career Planning Worksheet

Name _____ Date _____

Reviewed by: _____

1. <u>Short-Range Interests</u>

_____

_____

_____

_____

_____

My reasons for these interests are: (strengthen weakness, utilize strengths, etc.)

_____

_____

_____

_____

_____

Of these, I think I am most interested in the following one(s):

_____

_____

_____

_____

_____

2. <u>Long-Range Interests</u>

In addition to my short-range interests, I have long-range interests in these kinds of assignments:

_____

_____

_____

_____

_____

My reasons for these interests are:

_____

_____

_____

_____

_____

Of these, I think I am most interested in the following one(s):

_____

_____

_____

_____

_____

3. Personal Consideration

As I think about the effects that a change of assignment might have on my personal, off-the-job situation, I see the following as being important for my employer to know:

_____

_____

_____

_____

_____

4. Interests in a Particular Assignment

As I think of myself in a "line" assignment, my feelings are:

_____

_____

_____

_____

_____

As I think of myself in a "staff" assignment, my feelings are:

_____

_____

_____

_____

_____

In summary, my feelings regarding a "line" assignment versus a "staff" assignment (for me) are:

_____

_____

_____

_____

_____

5. In addition to all my comments in this form, I would like to say:

_____

_____

_____

_____

_____

Chapter Seven

PREPARING FOR THE PERFORMANCE APPRAISAL

The next five chapters are about the performance appraisal. This chapter is on getting ready for it. The next two deal with the definitions of performance, followed by a chapter on the performance appraisal itself. How to talk about the performance appraisal after it has been completed is the subject of the final of these chapters. The performance appraisal is the foundation of the development process. It is critical that an employee understand what her manager thinks of her performance and understand her strengths and needs improvements areas. This analysis will help her decide what and how to develop. It is very important to both the manager and the employee that the performance appraisal is set up correctly. To set up expectations appropriately, definitions of acceptable performance should be discussed before the appraisal can be done. The purpose of this chapter is to make sure all the key steps prior to the appraisal are done as well as possible.

Since the performance appraisal is the foundation of development, the proper preparation for this event is very important. It may seem easy to get ready for an appraisal but, in actuality, it is not an easy process. Even senior managers who have been through several get anxious beforehand. Some anxiety is good—it shows that the person cares; but too much anxiety can lead to too much sensitivity. The manager and employee need to relax and listen to each other as best they can. If the proper preparation is done, the chance for a very successful performance appraisal increases dramatically.

The outline in **Figure 7** gives a detailed step-by-step process with key actions in **Preparing for the Performance Appraisal.** The first step is to set a date for the discussion—at least 5 days ahead of the date of the appraisal. This gives the employee time to think about the appraisal and to prepare the appropriate information. The employee—especially a new one—needs to understand what the performance appraisal is for and what the intent of the meeting is. The next step is to give her a blank copy of the appraisal form and ask her to do a self-appraisal at the same time as the manager is doing his appraisal of her.

The employee and the manager must do their homework before they do the appraisal. The first step is to review the Job Definition and then to review the details of the Expectations Sharing exercise that they completed together. Many times there are detailed Goals that have been set up and agreed to at the beginning of the year or at the beginning of an assignment. All of these documents must be reviewed prior to the performance appraisal to make sure the details of the job definition, expectations, and goals are followed up on.

The key to a good performance appraisal is to set the correct tone. An employee will be more relaxed and productive in the meeting if he knows that the manager's intent is to help him grow and develop. This does not mean to minimize or to gloss over problems. The intent of a good development plan is to look for the problems and try to correct them. Looking for the strengths and trying to utilize them is also the key to a good performance appraisal. It is important in this step to continue to focus on the key issues and look at the broad view. It is equally important to stay away from nit-picking issues and make sure the discussion is based on a pattern of problems and not just one incident of a problem. The emphasis should be on what is not working and what can be done to improve the problem so the employee can be more productive and the organization can benefit from his greater effectiveness.

The final step in the preparation is documentation. It is important to get as many details as possible in writing. It may be easy to know an employee's strengths and weaknesses because you work with him every day. However, when a manager is in a meeting with the employee, and there are questions, a manager with little or no details and examples to back up her key points might easily miss some of those points. It is very helpful to pick two or three key points on the positive side and also in the needs improvement areas. It always helps to provide backup details and examples. Finally, keep the mindset focused on the idea that the performance appraisal is good for the employee and good for the company. This process should be looked forward to and not dreaded. A well-managed performance appraisal session will energize most employees. Even most employees with problems can leave the session feeling good since they better understand their problems now and have started to work on an improvement plan.

Preparing for the Performance Discussion
Figure 7

Notify employee of purpose, date, time, and location of the session

- o Give employee 5–10 days' lead time
- o Give employee a copy of the Performance Evaluation forms and ask him/her to evaluate their work and complete the forms prior to the discussion (self-evaluation)
- o Request that the employee review his/her job description and previously set goals/objectives to use as a basis for the self-evaluation
- o Request that the employee come prepared to discuss his/her:
    - accomplishments
    - concerns or problems—possible causes and solutions
    - professional development—things he/she would like to learn and do in the future

Review employee's performance data

- o Review previously set goals/objectives
- o Assemble quantity/quality/time measures of <u>results</u> related to employee's goals/objectives. Refer to any documentation you have such as notes or a performance log, and reports prepared by the employee
- o Focus on the overall picture by identifying key strengths and areas of development needed

Summarize the data and fill out the evaluation form

- o Determine "rating" of each criterion and overall rating
- o Prepare written comments that summarize accomplishments and areas for improvement—cite specific examples

Plan the Performance Evaluation discussion

- o Decide how you will get the employee involved in the discussion
- o Prepare notes for the discussion which include:
    - key strengths/accomplishments
    - major areas for improvement (note specific problems—causes, solutions, action steps)
    - ideas for future professional development
- o Prepare suggested follow-up plans for future goal setting, etc.

Chapter Eight

DEFINING GOOD PERFORMANCE

Many people believe that they know good performance when they see it. They seem to know what bad performance is. It may be possible to identify excellent performance and terrible performance but the definitions are usually unclear and inconsistent. Sometimes managers can pick out good performance, but it is helpful to have a definition of it, and also of poor performance. The purpose of this chapter is to try and help the manager and the employee to define what good—and bad—performance is.

The key elements of leadership are the first place to start the discussion, which is defined in **Figure 8**. Leadership drives any organization. Without good leadership, the organization will have difficulty achieving its goals. Leadership is not only in the management of an organization—a good organization has leadership throughout. The rest of this chapter attempts to define outstanding performance, good performance, acceptable performance, and needs improvement performance. These four definitions are listed in **Figure 9** and described below.

Leadership in an organization is very difficult to define. This book tries to describe it in four key elements. The first key definition of a leader in an organization is a person that **Delivers Results**. Organizations are set up to deliver results, to achieve their goals on a timely basis. In most cases, if the results are not delivered the organization will not survive. So without the results being delivered as needed, the other three key elements described in **Figure 8** will not matter. In order to deliver the results necessary for the organization to grow, or even survive, someone in the organization has to **Initiate Concepts**.

All organizations must initiate concepts. A creative organization obviously must come up with new products and ideas all the time. An information technology company must come up with new programs or solutions to customer problems. Even a grind-it-out organization must distinguish itself from its competitors. The best way to do this is to develop new ideas and concepts and make the organization better in some way. The best organizations have people in all areas who consistently initiate concepts.

The future of an organization depends on many elements. It must deliver the results and initiate concepts, but it must also take care of its people and make sure that they grow. Taking care of the people in an organization will help carry the organization into the future. A good leader recognizes that people are the key to an effective organization and **Leads and Develops** them so the organization can grow with the people necessary. The final key element of a good leader is her ability to **Work Across Organizational Boundaries**. Every organization is made up of parts. There is an accounting department, usually an operations team, a sales team, and several other teams that make up the whole. A leader works effectively with and across these distinct groups, bringing them together to work as one.

The chart in **Figure 9** describes the key elements of performance in the Performance Definitions as summarized below:

- The key to **Outstanding Performance** is consistency. A top person is someone who can be counted on all the time. An organization has a lot of continual challenges and the best people in that organization are the ones who are considered the "go to" people. A "go to" person gets that name by consistently delivering on the result he is asked to produce. This outstanding person needs little or no supervision and implements plans that are complex.

- The **Good Performer** delivers results and frequently does more than is expected but may not deliver on everything, every time. A good performer also needs little or no supervision and is probably asked to be a resource by many people in many circumstances. The good performer is asked to work on the moderately complex projects and maybe does not get assigned the most complex projects.

- **Acceptable Performers** are very important to an organization. In many organizations, the acceptable performer is the person who keeps the organization going day in and day out. This person does what is routinely expected of her and achieves acceptable results within a defined scope of responsibilities. She gets along with co-workers, implements routine plans, and handles normal responsibilities.

- An employee that **Needs Improvement** can stay in the organization if he shows signs of improving. He must be viewed as being able to work his way out of the needs improvement category in a reasonable timeframe. If the needs improvement person cannot work his way out of that category, he might not be a fit for the organization and may have to leave it. This employee routinely fails to deliver on what he is asked to do. A supervisor has to spend an inordinate amount of time watching over this person to make sure he does what is necessary. He is consistently unable to plan or implement routine projects.

Leadership Definitions
Figure 8

Delivers Results

Consistently achieves measurable business results that stand out in view of the circumstances: turning around key business trends from failing to succeeding; changing the course of things for the better by solving a major problem; managing to get good results in a variety of areas at the same time; and broadly delivering results in ways that build the business. Examples of results: cost-related items; quality improvement/assurance; completion of significant projects; improved customer service; and improvement of the organization safety performance and personnel development systems, etc.

Establishes an appropriate strategy for organization improvement and change and demonstrates satisfactory progress against objectives. Achieves an appropriate balance of building the organization and building the business.

Initiates Concepts

Takes a strategic viewpoint. Does not let current thinking be restricted by the past or by the apparent boundaries of own bailiwick. Anticipates significant trends and impending trouble. Shows initiative and skill in penetrating own part of the business to gain a firm understanding of what the problems are and why. Boils things down to those few key issues or opportunities that are most likely to have a major impact on the business. Identifies opportunities for innovation, devises fresh methods, and creates different approaches to existing opportunities. Comes up with concepts which address key issues, such as a strategy for organizational change, and which fuel business growth over the long term or benefit several parts of the company. Sponsors change efforts by others. Develops well-conceived, commonsense plans for putting concepts into action.

Operates Across Organizational Boundaries

Understands how to get things done within the company. Shows unusual breadth in working productively across company disciplines to get concepts and plans implemented. Commits self and work team to operate as effective members of the business team. Demonstrates persistence and skill in influencing people to collaborate in accomplishing a goal. Reaches out to make good use of all resources and expertise available. Demonstrates tenacity in getting complex programs into operation, in spite of barriers.

Leads and Develops People

Works in a positive, productive way with all people. Sets high performance standards. Focuses the attention of people on those few key things which can impact the business. Demonstrates the ability to recruit, train, and develop people, e.g., by setting goals and meeting them. Gets people to operate up to their capacity and as members of a team. Recognizes and nurtures strengths in others, even when these differ from own. Makes genuine progress on affirmative action commitments. Develops people to the point where they come up with their own ways to impact the business. Has a record of producing promotable people. Works on personal skill development and seeks to acquire broader knowledge of own and related business functions.

Evaluation Definitions

Figure 9

Outstanding

- Does the employee consistently achieve excellent results within broad scope of work?

- Does the employee routinely do more than is expected?

- Rarely needs coaching or supervision, even in new situations?

- Develops teamwork in achieving goals and fulfilling responsibilities?

- Demonstrates ability to plan and implement complex projects?

Acceptable

- Does the employee consistently achieve acceptable results within designated scope of work?

- Does what is expected and required?

- Cooperates with co-workers on request?

- Demonstrates ability to plan and implement routine projects?

Good

- Does the employee consistently achieve strong results within broad scope of work?

- Frequently does more than is expected?

- Needs minimum coaching and supervision in new situations?

- Is the employee sought as a resource by co-workers and colleagues?

- Demonstrates ability to plan and implement moderately complex projects?

Needs Improvement

- Does the employee sometimes fail to achieve expected results within designated scope of work?

- Occasionally fails to meet expectations or requirements?

- Requires coaching and supervision in routine situations?

- Occasionally fails to cooperate with co-workers and colleagues on request?

- Has difficulty planning and implementing routine projects?

Chapter Nine

THE PERFORMANCE APPRAISAL

The performance appraisal is the foundation to continuous improvement in people. In order to improve and to keep improving, people need feedback on their performance; they need—and want—to know what is working and what is not. The first step is for management to determine what the **Key Factors** are in their work environment. The performance appraisal in **Figure 10** is an example of a performance appraisal that works in many environments but not all. The management team should get together at the beginning of the employee development process and determine the top key factors that lead to achievement in his work environment. Picking ten key factors is about the right amount because it describes a manageable amount of performance elements but is not too many. An employee can keep ten key factors in his short-term memory and always know what his management is expecting of him.

The **Performance Appraisal** in **Figure 10** lists 10 key factors and their descriptions for consideration. These ten proposed key factors for work success are listed below with a short description of what they are and why they are important.

1. **Drive to Do Things Well** – Most organizations need a team of people willing to put in the effort, time, and energy to achieve the result necessary—no matter how long it takes. These overachievers are necessary in every organization and they should be recognized for their willingness to do whatever it takes.

2. **Setting Expectations and Confronting Problems and Issues** – Communication is critical in all organizations. Figuring out what

is expected and communicating those expectations is just as critical, or even more critical, than general communications. It is very important for all managers and supervisors to set expectations and communicate them, but this action is not only for managers and supervisors—everyone in an organization has expectations of the people they work with. The sooner a team of employees starts to communicate expectations amongst themselves, the better the team will function. Deviations from expectations or problems must be confronted in order to keep the team performing at a high level. The employee or manager who confronts the problem or issue in the most constructive and positive manner should get the highest rating in this area since her action helps everyone.

3. **Setting Priorities, Problem Solving & Decision Making** – Every organization has more to do than they have time to do it. The people in the organization and the management need to constantly set priorities, make decisions, and solve problems. A high performance organization needs everyone to have the ability to problem solve, set priorities, and make good decisions. As long as management has set the foundation of clear expectations and principles, the decisions should be made as close to the problem as possible. The managers or employees who can set priorities, make good decisions, and solve problems need to get the highest rating.

4. **Being Open, Honest and Fair with Others** – Almost all organizations rely on a team to achieve the necessary results. A team functions best when the people on it are open, honest, and fair with each other. The more the people in the team show these characteristics and demonstrate them with each other, the less time is wasted on team politics and the more productive the team can be.

5. **Developing Group and Individual Effectiveness** – All managers need skills for developing the team—and each of the individuals on their team—or they are not managers. The definition of a manager is one who leads his team. If a manager does not demonstrate these leadership and development skills, he is not much of a manager. The employee team members should also demonstrate these skills. The more people on the team who are contributing to its development and to the individual development of their teammates, the

better the chance that the team will be successful in accomplishing its goals. A good manager rewards the members who help him to develop and achieve the goals of the team.

6. **Communication Skills** – Every person on every team needs to have good communication skills. A good argument can be made that this is one of the top skills of every person on the team. Maybe the communication skill is second only to the technical skill requirements. A good business will value this skill highly and make sure that every employee gets training in communication. Written and oral communication skills will be needed in most organizations.

7. **Knowing Their Skills and Weaknesses and Seeking to Improve** – The definition of continuous improvement is finding the skills available and using them to achieve the goal while seeking to continually improve. The same is true for people. A person who understands her strengths and weaknesses and is constantly seeking to improve is going to be much more effective in the future. Many employees can grow by trying to continually improve, and they can pass high achievers that came into the organization with higher skills. An organization which has a majority of people who know their strengths and weaknesses and are striving to keep improving is better positioned to meet the challenges of the future.

8. **Ideas and Change** – The engine that drives an organization to improve and grow is the generation and development of ideas and innovation. An organization needs to find its key innovators and help them to develop their skills. Many organizations stymie these employees by definition. Most employees are trying to be organized and get their priorities done as soon as possible. Many times the great innovators or the people that generate the revolutionary ideas are the employees that may not be constantly focused on efficiency. These idea generators need to be found, encouraged, and protected—especially in a developed, creative business. All employees need to be rated on this category since ideas and the ability to effect change is important in the entire organization. The best idea-generators need to be found, but all employees need to be encouraged to generate good ideas and be recognized for their results.

9. **Broad & Long-Range View** – The higher a person is in an organization the more important this skill is for both the individual and the organization to be effective. Most effective organizations have people at the top levels thinking about the long-term future and the perspective of the broad view of that organization. Every organization, big or small, needs to have the future in mind or there will not be one. Most employees do not need these skills, but they will need them if they want to grow within the organization. All high potential employees will need to demonstrate this skill before they are ever promoted to senior levels. It is important to start early in an employee's career to identify whether or not she has this vision for future development.

10. **Understanding the Technical Aspects** – Every employee needs to have the technical skills to do his job. If he is not qualified to do it, he either needs more training, needs to change jobs internally, or he needs to leave the organization. The best way to have qualified employees is to have, first, a good hiring program, and, then, one for training. As it is both difficult and expensive to terminate an employee, it makes better business sense to train the under-qualified employee rather than to let him go. Also, the fact that an employee has good technical skills does not mean he is successful. He needs to have the technical skills first, but if he doesn't have the drive, if he cannot communicate with others, if he cannot make good decisions…and the list goes on and on. Results are the key to a successful organization. All the knowledge and skills in the world mean nothing if they don't translate into **Results.**

Coaching for Excellence Figure 10

Name: _____

Department: _____ Title: _____

Review Period from: _____ to: _____ Date of Hire: _____ Date of Review: _____

1. DRIVE TO DO THINGS WELL; WILLINGNESS TO PUT FORTH THE EFFORT NEEDED • Having the personal drive and determination to make things happen and to get results. Willingness to give what it takes to do the job. Taking pride in accomplishments. Wanting to do the best job possible on each assignment. Getting things done—not giving up.	____ Not yet observed ____ Numerical rating Supporting examples/data _____ _____ _____
2. SETTING EXPECTATIONS AND STANDARDS AND CONFRONTING PROBLEM SITUATIONS AND ISSUES • Clearly communicating expectations and standards. Ability to let others know what is expected of them and why. Confronting situations which need correction. Facing issues head on with the ability to work through them.	____ Not yet observed ____ Numerical rating Supporting examples/data _____ _____ _____
3. SETTING PRIORITIES; PROBLEM SOLVING; DECISION-MAKING • Skillfully setting priorities among items demanding attention. Making sound, well-thought-out decisions. Ability to sort through symptoms and zero in on the real problem. Organizing and planning time in order to get things done. Efficient use of time management skills.	____ Not yet observed ____ Numerical rating Supporting examples/data _____ _____ _____
4. BEING OPEN, HONEST AND FAIR WITH OTHERS • Earning the trust and confidence of others. Being straightforward, open, and honest. Taking time to listen and understand what others say. Treating people equally and fairly. Being objective, fair, and understanding across racial and sexual lines.	____ Not yet observed ____ Numerical rating Supporting examples/data _____ _____ _____

	Not yet observed / Numerical rating / Supporting examples/data
5. DEVELOPING GROUP AND INDIVIDUAL EFFECTIVENESS • Involving people in setting objectives. Developing group effectiveness and team spirit. Recognizing the knowledge and skills of employees and increasing their attributes through effective coaching and instructing.	_____ Not yet observed _____ Numerical rating Supporting examples/data _____ _____ _____
6. COMMUNICATION SKILLS • Communicating well with people on all levels. Conveying ideas persuasively and convincingly so others can understand. Ability to listen to others.	_____ Not yet observed _____ Numerical rating Supporting examples/data _____ _____ _____
7. KNOWING PERSONAL STRENGTHS AND WEAKNESSES AND SEEKING TO IMPROVE • Having a good understanding of self. Ability to assess personal strengths and weaknesses accurately. Accepting constructive criticism and feedback and doing something about it. Having a strong sense of personal direction.	_____ Not yet observed _____ Numerical rating Supporting examples/data _____ _____ _____

8. BROAD, LONG-RANGE PERSPECTIVE • Making it a practice to do long-range planning to prepare for the future. Having a broad view of the work. Ability to see the "bigger picture."	_____ Not yet observed _____ Numerical rating Supporting examples/data _____ _____ _____
9. IDEAS AND CHANGE • Improving the operation through change. Generating new ideas and finding ways to do things better.	_____ Not yet observed _____ Numerical rating Supporting examples/data _____ _____ _____
10. UNDERSTANDING THE TECHNICAL ASPECTS OF WORK • Having a basic understanding of the technical aspects of the job. Having enough technical ability to understand the equipment and the process.	_____ Not yet observed _____ Numerical rating Supporting examples/data _____ _____ _____

Chapter Ten

DISCUSSING STRENGTHS & PERFORMANCE PROBLEMS

It is just as important to discuss performance successes as it is to discuss problems. Discussing the success of an employee over the last year should be a lot easier than discussing the problems and the needs improvement areas. Most of the time managers dig right into the problems and gloss over success. This approach puts the employee immediately on the defensive and hurts her overall confidence. The tone can suddenly shift from a discussion on continuous development to a discussion on how she needs to defend her problem areas. The situation can become even worse and she can start to hide these problems from her manager. Setting the tone from the beginning of the performance appraisal will help her to stay at ease. The intent of the meeting will be more easily achieved in a relaxed environment. The purpose of this chapter is to discuss some guidelines to a successful performance appraisal meeting. Discussing the positive and the negative aspects of the employee's performance over the last year will be important to setting the tone. The chapter starts with some general guidelines on discussing the positive achievements over the last year and then it goes into the more difficult topic of **Performance Problems**. The guidelines in **Figure 11** help outline some key points for the discussion on Performance Problems.

An employee is almost always nervous at the beginning of a performance appraisal, even if he has had a good year with some strong successes. Even senior people have problems hearing about the things that they need to improve on. The key to making a performance appraisal a constructive meeting that focuses on the continuous improvement of the employee is to get him to relax and be open and receptive.

(Sometimes the tone of the performance appraisal needs to be totally different than a continuous improvement plan. An employee might not be a fit for the job or organization, and then the intent of the meeting is progressive discipline or a discussion that leads to discharge. This type of discussion is not within the scope of this book, and gaining an understanding of the steps to effective progressive discipline may require research from other sources.)

Setting the tone of the performance appraisal meeting begins with telling the employee the intent of the meeting. An employee will be much more likely to listen to constructive criticism if she knows that the manager's **intent is to help her grow and develop** and not to find fault with her. The meeting should start with the positive aspects of her performance over the last year. Try to describe her wins but be careful not to sugarcoat the issues. A good employee just wants to know the truth about her performance so she can improve her problems and utilize her strengths. The strengths are very important to discuss so that an employee knows she is a valuable contributor to the team and that her hard work is appreciated. It will probably be much easier to discuss her strengths than her needs improvements areas, but it is helpful to use the following guidelines for delivering the intended message on the employee's best skills.

Guidelines for Discussing an Employee's Strengths

- Be honest, don't just try and say something positive.
- Be clear and direct. Make sure the employee understands the key points.
- Ask the employee to repeat what he heard.
- Use examples. Try to find objective examples with backup results.
- Try to limit the list of top strengths to 3-5, so that he can really understand the key strengths.
- Leave time for him to discuss how he can grow his strengths. A top rating—even on a strength—might be grade inflation if it is unjustified and will not be as helpful as the manager's intent.

- Discuss how the employee can use his strengths to help the team or company even more.
- Talk about why these skills are beneficial to the organization.
- Ask the employee if there are any questions or concerns. He might have more questions than the manager estimated and it will be good for the manager to take the time to listen and clarify everything.
- Come prepared to discuss the positives. Do your homework here also. An employee who understands his strengths and knows how to use them to enhance the team will be a very powerful force in helping the organization achieve its goals in the upcoming year.

The next step in the employee development process is the hardest step of all. The manager or supervisor is advised to spend the appropriate time to prepare for this very important upcoming meeting. **Figure 11** helps to identify the key steps in **Preparing to Discuss Performance Problems.**

The chart in **Figure 11** is divided into three columns. The first column lists four key actions to take under the heading of **"What to do."** These four topics will help the manager understand some of the critical actions required in discussing performance problems. There might be several other actions that a manager might want to take. The next column describes why these first four actions are important and the column is titled simply **"Why it is done."** This column explains why these actions will help get the desired result. The final column helps the manager by giving some examples of what to say and how to organize his thoughts. This column is titled **"How it can be said or done."** The purpose of this column is to try and give the manager some exact wordage to help him get started on what he might want to say to the employee. This approach is very helpful to all managers but especially new mangers. This area will give him a first step in trying to talk about a very difficult topic—the employee's needs improvement areas.

The best way to understand this chart in **Figure 11** is to use an example to get the right point across and make the chart easy to use. The following is a step-by-step example of how to discuss a performance problem by using **Figure 11.**

Step by step instructions on how to discuss a performance problem using Figure 11:

Step 1 – Select 2-3 key areas that need improvement from the performance appraisal.

Step 2 – Use the first column in **Figure 11**, titled "**What to do.**" The first item says: "Describe the employee's specific performance." An example might be that she does not **Confront Problem Situations and Issues** from number 2 in the **Figure 10** performance appraisal (See **Chapter 9**). The suggestion here is to be specific, clear, and tie the comments back to the performance appraisal.

Step 3 – There are two reasons given for **being specific** in column 2. The first reason is that the employee might not be aware of the problem. This might be the first time she hears about it. (It is always interesting to see if the employee listed the same problem areas in her self-performance appraisal). The second reason to be specific is that it will probably minimize the amount of defensiveness and argument.

Step 4 – The final step in this process is to use specific language. Being clear can really help the manager be effective and get the intended points across. The third column in **Figure 11** gives an example of how the manager can phrase his comments on the employee's performance. Using the example in **Step 2**, above, on the lack of confronting problem situations and issues, the manager might say the following to the employee: "**You need to identify and address problems in a more timely manner. The subordinate's tardiness was not confronted until it was out of control.**"

The manager wants to clearly explain to the employee, in this example, that she is not meeting expectations and needs to improve her confrontational skills. The manager could use the example in **column 3**, and say, "**There is one area that I would like to discuss. I am concerned about your ability to confront problem situations and issues.**" The next step is for the manager to be specific and clear about what he means. He could next say, "**I have noticed that you had problems with other employees 4 times and never said anything. You waited until their performance became a huge problem, you were angry, and finally confronted the problem. By the time you said**

something, you were so upset that you raised your voice and your language was inappropriate."

The language given above was specific and included examples. It could have been even better by stating a specific incident, like mentioning the date and the exact conversation that the manager had heard. The chart in **Figure 11** is an example of **what *not* to say**. In this instance, the manager might be saying **"You never say anything about other people's problems unless you get mad."** A statement like this is not specific enough and will probably lead to the employee getting defensive. The conversation could easily switch from a conversation on how to help the employee grow to one where the manager and employee are arguing about the employee's performance.

Discussing an employee's performance can be very difficult, especially the problem areas. This might be one of the most difficult conversations a manager has in his career. He is nervous and so is the employee. He might say the wrong thing, or the conversation might just start badly and go downhill from there. A poorly managed performance appraisal conversation might have the opposite effect than the manager intended. A conversation intended to help the employee use his strengths and work on his needs improvement areas might end up creating a problem between the manager and employee.

The guidelines for helping a manager give an effective performance appraisal will assist them in getting the intended points across, and, so, to continuously develop their employees, their team, and the entire organization.

Guide to Discussing Performance Problems Figure 11

Steps for discussing performance problems with employees:

What you do	Why it's done	How it can be said or done
o Describe the employee's specific performance.	Employee may be unaware of his/her behavior.	"There is one area that I would like to discuss. I am concerned about...."
	A specific performance statement reduces arguments.	*Non-Specific* "You make too many errors!" (What is too many?) "You're usually late!" *More specific:* "There were 6 errors made on the January report."
o Describe the expected standard of performance	If we can't state exactly what is required, how is the employee going to know what satisfactory performance is?	"The required performance..... (be specific)."
o Ask employee to identify cause of the situation.	Employee identification, of course, helps in later acceptance of solution. Employee may see causes not seen by the leader. Identifying the most probable causes increases the quality of the solutions. Keep discussion focused on causes to prevent premature focus on solutions.	"What do you think is the cause of this situation?" "What other causes do you see?"

What you do	Why it's done	How it can be said or done
o Ask employee for his/her suggested solutions and discuss.	If employee is going to play a role in changes needed, then it is better to gain acceptance by guiding him/her to determine the solution. The leader may have ideas or suggestions based on general knowledge or experience which can improve the quality of the solution. The leader and employee explore each solution in order to arrive at a solution that will correct the problem. The leader should, if possible, encourage the employee to select the solutions that will be implemented.	"What suggestions do you have for increased performance?" "What do you think of this idea?" In response to: "I'll try harder": "What would be required to do that?" "What resources are available to you?" "Are there any special problems in doing that?" "What do you see as the best solution?" "Why do you feel that is the best solution?"

Chapter Eleven

DEVELOPING AN IMPROVEMENT PLAN

The expectations are now clear to the employee. The job description is now clear to the employee. The strengths and needs improvements are now clear to the employee—and the employee knows how he performed over the last year. The next step is to begin the preparation for the upcoming year. The two final steps in the overall process are to **Develop an Improvement Plan** and to **Develop Goals** for the next year. The next two chapters focus on these two areas. The purpose of this chapter is to develop the improvement plan using all the information generated prior to this step.

This chapter has two figures to help facilitate in the development of an improvement plan. **Figure 12** gives a list of suggested guidelines, and **Figure 13** is a form to organize the key information necessary. Such a plan can help the employee continuously develop. This chapter will show how all the work getting to this point will help the manager and employee develop an easy-to-use and effective plan.

The guideline in **Figure 12** has 6 key elements. The first two suggestions speak to developing the plan jointly, with both manager and employee totally involved, using the information developed in the performance appraisal. The next two suggestions are to focus on the details of the improvement plan by gathering specifics about what needs improving. The more specific the information, the better the planning process. The last two suggestions are presented to help the manager and employee hone in on two of the three most important improvement areas. A balance should be struck between gathering as much information as possible and concentrating it into a succinct and operable plan.

Figure 13 is the form that can be used to put the entire improvement plan together into a presentable format. There are 6 key steps in developing the plan. The following steps will guide the manager and employee in filling out the form, and, more importantly, in developing a plan for the employee to improve.

Step 1 – Select 2-3 key areas that the manager and the employee have agreed to work on over the next year. The key to selecting the right areas of improvement is to pick the areas that need the most improvement, or the areas that would help the team the most.

Step 2 – Since the employee and the manager agreed on the 2-3 areas necessary for the improvement plan, there must have been a reason for selecting these specific areas. Everyone knows why these areas were selected and they will not be forgotten easily. However, 6 months from the appraisal date, the reasons for selecting certain improvement areas will not be as clear. Listing the justification will also help complete answers to the next steps.

Step 3 – The next step is to dream about the possibilities and list the desired end result. The final end result may not be possible in the next year but it will help the employee know where she wants to be when she has ultimately achieved her long-term goal. The action steps over the next year or even longer will be easier to develop with the vision of this end point kept in mind.

Step 4 – This step is really the core of the improvement plan. The clearer the actions that need to be developed, the easier they will be to implement. So, the goal here is to be action-oriented and focused on actions that can be taken. The actions can be: 1) taking a class, 2) getting a tutor, 3) having a mentor help, 4) practicing a new behavior, 5) getting coaching from an expert, 6) shadowing another employee to see how he is successful, 7) going online and finding the appropriate information (this could be by the immediate fruits of a web search or by taking a class online), 8) reading a book or magazine on the information…the list goes on and on.

Step 5 – An employee cannot achieve the expected improvement without some support. If an organization is truly committed to continuous employee improvement, this is the place where it can show its commitment. Every action step will need some support. It may be as simple as asking the manager to provide coaching on the improvement areas throughout the year. The employee might need some time off for classes. The organization might need to take a risk and let the employee try some new skills in a non-threatening way. The employee might even have to change jobs.

Step 6 – The employee knows where she wants to be. She has action steps identified to help her be successful. She has listed the support she needs to make progress. This final step in developing the improvement plan is to identify what success looks like. An employee will be much more successful and motivated in implementing her improvement action steps if she knows what success looks like and what she can do to help the team.

Guidelines in Developing an Improvement Plan
Figure 12

Some key points to keep in mind

- Plan is jointly developed and agreed to by both parties.
- Feedback shared during the performance appraisal is a source of information from which to extract themes relating to major strengths and areas for development.
- Action steps should be specific and clearly defined and should have easily measured endpoints.
- Timelines should be defined for each step.
- Plan should cover areas where improvement is most needed.
- It is advantageous to key on one or two areas.

Improvement Plan

Figure 13

AREA FOR IMPROVEMENT	JUSTIFICATION FOR PRIORITY	PERSONAL GOAL
ACTION STEPS	SUPPORT NEEDED	MEASURE OF SUCCESS

Chapter Twelve

GOAL SETTING

There are two sets of goals that will usually be developed at the beginning of every year. A person will set the goals that he wants to achieve in his organization throughout the upcoming year. He will also develop goals on how he wants to improve his own skills during that time. Most often, these goals will overlap. A person might have 5-6 goals for the year on what he will accomplish at work. These will usually be goals like improving sales by 5%, or reducing costs by 8%, and so forth. He will usually have 1-2 major goals on how he will improve his own skills and performance. These personal goals will be something like taking a writing class, learning how to budget, or talking to a team member right away if there is a conflict. There are many organizational goals and these are usually used for a bonus plan or gain-sharing plan. Most organizations that are committed to developing their people will require a goals-setting plan for their employees so that they have goals to continuously improve. Many times these two goal-setting plans overlap, or the personal goals are rolled into the organization's goals for the employee. The purpose of this chapter is to show how an employee can develop overall goals for the year which combine the professional with the personal. The idea is to develop one set of major goals for the person for the upcoming year. This plan of combining goals should help the employee manage his year better and help the manager to oversee her progress more easily. Of course there is a form to help in this area also. (See **Figure 14.**)

An employee who has developed the plan from **Chapter Eleven** is already more than halfway done with Chapter Twelve. The first step in this chapter is to take the areas for improvement listed in Chapter Eleven, select the top two areas of improvement, and transfer them into the chart in **Figure 14**. For example, the employee and manager agree that the two most important areas for the employee to improve are his writing skills and his conflict resolution skills. Both of these sets of skills are very important for the employee to improve in so that he can achieve better results in the future—or even as preparation for a future promotion.

The first goal is very important for development and future results—but not as important as the organization's needs for results in the present. The employee lists 6 goals for the upcoming year. The goals have a high weighting factor to reflect their overall importance to the organization.

These goals are work results relating to the employee's day-to-day responsibilities. These goals will usually have a 15-25% weighting factor that shows that they are critical. These goals will usually be in the **Goal Areas** of Sales, Production, Finance, Marketing, Research, etc. They are usually goals that are objective in nature and are time-bounded (with deadlines) and measurable at the end of the year. A couple of examples are listed below.

Weight	Goal Area	Goal Statement	Resources Needed
25%	Sales	To increase sales revenue by 5% over last year by landing 2 new accounts.	Manager to travel on two new sales calls.
15%	Customer Service	Retain 95% of the present customers' business by visiting them at least once per month.	Customer Service to follow up on all calls.

The goals listed above are good examples of realistic yet challenging ones that are very important to the organization this year. There are usually 3-4 of these important, results-oriented goals for every person in an organization. They are critical to every organization's survival. Also critical are goals for the development of the individuals within the organization—especially in the organization that is genuinely committed to its employees and their growth. This development lays the foundation not only for the organization's long-term success, but also for the employees' who will now be trained for the future.

The next step in this process is for the employee to finish her goals-setting by taking those improvement goals that were first discussed at the beginning of the chapter and applying them to the form in **Figure 14**. These goals will probably have a lower weighting factor and they might even be less objective in nature. However, they might be just as important to the future of the company if they are selected correctly and implemented well.

Setting the personal improvement goals is a very difficult process because it is very difficult to know what skills an employee might need in the future. It is also difficult to know how to improve her skills in certain areas since adults learn by doing and not every skill comes from reading or the classroom.

However, if the manager and the employee put the right amount of time and thought into developing her improvement goals for continuous improvement, the new goals for the year will help her to be prepared for the future.

The following examples will assist the employee and the manager in developing the employee's goals.

Weight	Goal Area	Goal Statement	Resources Needed
15%	Personal Development	To improve writing skills by the end of the year. (Improvement will be measured by a performance appraisal with input from the managerand several co-workers).	Time off to take a writing class and tuition reimbursement.
10%	Personal Development	To improve conflict resolution skills throughout the year. (Improvement will be measured by quarterly reviews from the manager and the manager's manager)	Read a book on conflict resolution styles and techniques. Have a mentor assigned who is known as an expert in this area. Meet monthly with mentor. Try new skills in non-threatening environment once per month.

The final step in this part of the process is to have the employee and the manager sign the goals-setting sheet as a commitment among the two individuals to strive for and achieve these goals. These goals can also be used for a bonus plan as well as a development plan for future promotions. This is the plan for the year, but things always change in business. The employee and manager should be open to change, as necessary.

Goal Setting
Figure 14

Weight	Goal Area	Goal Statement	Resources Needed

Agreement to Goals:

_____   Date: _____   _____   Date: _____

(Employee's Signature)   (Supervisor's Signature)

Chapter Thirteen

DEVELOPMENT PLAN SUMMARY

This final chapter brings together and summarizes all of the topics that have previously been discussed. An organization that is committed to developing its people will reap rewards for many years. An organization that is sincere about helping its people grow is a very smart organization. People are very perceptive. If your employees see that you are interested in their future, they will work hard to make sure that the organization has a future. Is there a better motivator for an employee than to know he is important and that he is considered a part of the organization's future? If the managers and supervisors are really smart and they do their homework, they will come to understand the skills that an organization will need in the future. The question is, which is smarter and more cost effective, to train a present employee to get the skills of the future, or to go out on the street, find a loyal new employee who you think might have the right skills, and train him about the organization?

There is an old saying that it costs an organization a million dollars to find, interview, hire, and train the right employee. To train that employee to the point where he is contributing is a large part of the cost of getting a new employee. It costs a lot less than a million dollars to retrain a present employee. The development process that is the essence of this book is one way to do so. It may not even matter over time what method of development a manager chooses as long as it works. The key to development is making it happen. Your employees really are worth an investment since they do spend one quarter to one third of their lives at work!

One last form to deal with. You may at this stage not want to see one more form. You may want to walk away from the forms. But this last one may be the only one you really need. All the others are meant to be tools to help the supervisor or manager compile information to put on this last form. If an employee knows what his strengths are and has a plan to utilize those strengths, he will be much more productive at work. On the other side of the development process, if an employee knows what skills he needs to develop and has a solid plan to develop them, he will be a much more productive employee in the future. The purpose of this final form is to bring together all the information gathered over the 2-3 month development process into one easy-to-use form. (The first time with the entire process will require a couple hours per week over a 2-3 month timeframe; in subsequent years it will only take only a few hours over a month of minimal work).

The **Summary of the Development Plan** in **Figure 15** should be the summary of everything developed up to this point. It should be in a form that the manager can easily file and get access to; more importantly, it should be something that the employee can actually carry around with her every day. It should be only one page so she can pull it out at any time and see if she is making progress. It will also help her if she needs to use her best skills to solve a work problem or be more productive at work.

Figure 15 starts with the **Strengths Areas** which are usually easier for the manager and the employee to discuss. The best reference for this form is the Coaching for Excellence performance appraisal (see **Figure 10** in **Chapter Nine**). There are probably 4-5 strength areas mentioned in the completed employee's performance appraisal. It might be easier for the employee to always have the top three strengths on the top of his mind. Then, when he runs into an unexpected problem or challenge, he can quickly remind himself of the details of his best skills and this will probably help him in his problem solving. This action will increase his chance of meeting the challenge efficiently and effectively.

The next step is to think about some of those unexpected or difficult challenges that the employee might be faced with in the upcoming year, and plan ways to solve those problems. This is really contingency planning. If an employee can visualize a potential problem in the future, she can think of clever ways to solve it by using her strengths. She will be far more prepared to solve that problem in the future with a little planning. This is almost like a world class athlete before a competition. If she visualizes herself winning the competition, she is far more likely to achieve that goal.

Development Needs are always more challenging to discuss. Very few people like to hear where they need improvement. It is very difficult to really believe that a self-examination will identify problem areas. This will be especially difficult for a new employee—although discussing problem areas is actually just as difficult for the new manager because conflict avoidance is in us all. Some people think of fight or flight when they think about the potential conflict, but that should not be the issue here. If the manager sets the tone is set correctly, the purpose of the meeting will be clear. Identifying an employee's development needs is not meant to downgrade her or to make her defensive. The purpose of this process is to help the employee grow and develop. A person cannot grow if she does not know what her problem areas are.

The first step in summarizing the development needs is to go back to the performance appraisal and pick out the 2 or 3 areas that need the most improvement. Pick those improvement areas from the appraisal that really mean something. The form calls them "What Counts' Factors." The employee might not be good at a certain skill but if she doesn't need that skill now or in the foreseeable future, then the skill is not really a **"What Counts' Factor**. Pick a few (2-3) skills that are important to the employee and the organization and which would really make a difference to both.

The employee and the manager should work together closely on the next step: selecting action steps to improve the employee's needs improvement areas. Try very hard to focus on the real development needs here and pick action steps that will really help the employee improve. It is said that an adult might need a significant emotional event in order to change. That might be true for an adult who wants to change dramatically in a short period of time; however, the purpose of this process is continuous improvement. An employee who works hard with his manager to select developmental needs and then comes up with a good plan of action can successfully change and grow over time. An employee can grow and change if he has a good, simple plan he can remember and utilize—it could be summarized on a single piece of paper for easy reference. He can use this plan almost daily to improve his chances of success.

A development plan can help an employee continually grow and add new skills. An employee with new skills and a more positive attitude will be more productive. A more productive employee will help an organization be more successful. A more successful organization can reinvest in more employees. The more employees that are on the development cycle and become more productive, the better the chance the organization has for future success. This is the circle of life at work. If the circle of life is broken— employees stop developing new skills, their productivity does not increase—the organization will flounder.

Summary of the Development Plan
Figure 15

Strengths

"What Counts" Skills

1. _____

2. _____

3. _____

Action Plan Summary

1. _____

2. _____

3. _____

Development Needs

"What Counts" Development Areas

1. _____

2. _____

3. _____

Action Plan Summary

1. _____

2. _____

3. _____

Printed in the United States
83499LV00001B/208-528/A

9 781592 992829